The Kaufmann Mercantile Guide

THE KAUFMANN MERCANTILE GUIDE

HOW TO SPLIT WOOD, SHUCK AN OYSTER, AND MASTER OTHER SIMPLE PLEASURES

EDITED BY **Alexandra Redgrave** AND **Jessica Hundley**

PRINCETON ARCHITECTURAL PRESS · NEW YORK

CONTENTS

PREFACE

Before this book, there was a store. And before the store, there was a blog called *Kaufmann Mercantile*, which I started in 2009 while living in Los Angeles and working as a filmmaker. At the time, several of my friends were moving away from making film to make furniture. Being more hands on greatly appealed to me. I became interested in how things were made and how they could be maintained or fixed when broken.

Growing up in Germany, where the Green Party has influenced lawmaking for three decades, I had an early understanding of disposable consumerism and its negative effects on the environment. To me, the solutions offered by manufacturers and retailers, like using recycled plastic or green products, couldn't be the only way to improve the status quo. I felt there could be other, simpler solutions: making things yourself; using natural, sustainable materials or ingredients; designing products so they could be easily repaired; producing goods at such high quality, you'd never want to throw them away; or buying only the things you need—independently manufactured and created with care and craftsmanship.

There seemed to be no store with a clear and true focus on quality, so I decided to build one myself. Today, Kaufmann Mercantile searches the globe for the best products and makers out there, with the goal to set a new, better standard for retailers. We research each item in depth and speak with every maker directly to provide detailed information about all our products. From the beginning, our company has been motivated by that same love (or rather, obsession) for quality and by the mission to offer better tools and objects, those things that will truly enrich your everyday life. Since my first blog post—about the Estwing hammer, a trusted tool made in the United States since the 1930s—our editorial platform has grown alongside the store to become a resource for the mindful consumer, offering everything from how-to projects and the history of materials to profiles on pioneering designers and makers.

We're thrilled to now share some of our favorite discoveries and ideas in this book. Many thanks to the editors, Alexandra Redgrave and Jessica Hundley, for their amazing work. I hope you will enjoy reading and learning from the pages that follow. I'd love to hear about the things you make and fix and do—all the self-made adventures this book might inspire.

Sebastian Kaufmann
—

Write to me at:
sebastian@kaufmann-mercantile.com

INTRODUCTION

This book began out of a curiosity for how we grow, build, and craft the world around us. We discovered that there's an art to a simple task done well, from planting with the seasons to caring for cast iron. It calls for consideration and creativity—rolling up our sleeves and digging into the details. It means getting messy, and, perhaps, messing up, to experience the singular satisfaction of doing it yourself.

For guidance and inspiration, we turned to experts and enthusiasts, those wonderful people who dedicate their lives to a particular skill or take pleasure in the day-to-day endeavors that most of us leave to someone else. We also sought out the tools that not only help you get the job done but are a joy to use too.

Each of the how-tos that follow, then, is an opportunity to master the art of the everyday. Some you will use often, such as poaching an egg or securing a knot, while others might explore new territory. Knowing how to ford a stream, for example, requires one to first venture out into the wilderness, and the urge to save a plant's seed arises only after a garden has taken root.

As the book came together, we learned that everyone has their own way of doing things. We by no means want you to think *our* way is the *only* way. Therein lies the beauty of the how-to: the final result or the finished product can be as unique as the person who made it. In our world of modern convenience, doing it yourself is immensely rewarding. And so, consider the book in your hands as a starting point. We hope you, like us, find inspiration in these pages to experiment, to investigate, to create, and to make your everyday a little better.

Alexandra Redgrave and Jessica Hundley

ONE

Kitchen

HOW TO

—

CARE FOR CAST-IRON PANS

—

"If I could have only a single pan to cook with for the rest of my life, it would be made with cast iron. (I own six in varying sizes.) Cast-iron pans are highly effective, durable, and versatile, whether used on the stovetop or in the oven. Whenever I find old rusted ones in antique stores, I run them through an oven-clean cycle, scrub them down, and reseason them. Then they're as good as new."

—Michael Ruhlman, cookbook author

COOK WHILE THE IRON IS HOT

Thanks to a surface that heats up evenly and requires little oil for cooking—not to mention a high iron content that fortifies your food every time you cook on it—cast-iron pans are the workhorses of kitchenware. Still, the hardy material doesn't take care of itself any more than your dog neatly puts away his bowl. Herewith, a guide.

1   Unlike the slippery surface of Teflon and all the other nonstick chemicals that off-gas when heated, cast iron takes a bit more work to get to the optimal temperature. Put the pan on the stove over medium heat for a good three to five minutes until it's thoroughly heated. Then add your cooking oil or lard and throw on your ingredients.

2   An issue may, ahem, arise while cooking meat on cast iron: a pungent smell. It could be that the pan is too hot or wasn't cleaned well enough between uses. (If you don't fully rinse off the cooking fat and residue from the previous meal, it can start to burn and smoke.) To prevent your kitchen from smelling like old bacon, cook your meat on medium heat and, once you dish out the cooked ingredients, immediately run your pan under hot running water. (Cold water can potentially cause cracking or damage, as the outer layer of iron contracts faster than the inner core.) The thermal shock kicks off most of the residue and naturally rinses the surface of any oils.

→

3 If there are still remaining pieces of food, toss on about ½ cup of coarse salt and rub with a sponge. The rough texture of the salt removes excess oils and bits of food without compromising the pan's seasoning (the nonstick coating that naturally forms with use, creating a protective sheen). You can also use a scrubber brush with coarse bristles to loosen any food residue, then rinse again under hot water. No soap needed! In fact, even a little bit of soap could clean away the seasoning you've worked so hard to build up.

At some point you may want to reseason your cast-iron cookware, especially if food is sticking, the pan is looking dull, or maybe a relative left it soaking all night in the sink. (A little rust can be scoured away with steel wool before reseasoning.) Scrub your pan, dry it completely, and coat the surface inside and out with a thin layer of flaxseed oil, melted vegetable shortening, or vegetable oil. (Oils that oxidize easily, such as olive oil, will smoke.) Place a sheet of aluminum foil on the bottom rack of the oven to catch any drippings, and bake your pan at 400°F for an hour. Let it sit (with the oven turned off) until cooled. If you prefer, you can recoat the surface after each cleaning.

The Flax of Life

Flaxseed oil is great for maintaining cast-iron pans because it's an excellent sealant. Flaxseed produces a "drying oil," which transforms into a tough, protective film. This isn't drying in the sense of losing moisture through evaporation, however. (The term is actually a misnomer.) The transformation happens via a chemical process called polymerization. Similarly, linseed oil, the non-food-grade equivalent of flaxseed oil, is used by artists to produce high-quality oil paints that dry hard and glassy on the canvas, and by woodworkers to give their work a nice luster.

Natural-Bristle Pot Scrubber

Extracted from the fleshy leaves of the agave, tampico fibers (like the ones
used in this scrub brush) are resistant to most synthetic chemicals,
alkaline and acidic solutions, as well as heat. Traditionally, the fibers were used
by Native Americans to make durable ropes and mats. Here, the fibers are
stitched together with bronze wire and finished with a light yet incredibly strong
birch-wood handle. This simple brush will make quick work of all
sorts of tough cleanup jobs for many dinner parties and family meals to come.

SHUCK
AN OYSTER

—

"Shucking is one of those sneaky life skills that you may not use every day, but secretly take great pride in when you effortlessly pull it off. I can picture Ernest Hemingway with a cigar dangling out of his mouth and his sleeves rolled up, oyster knife glinting in the afternoon sun, dominating a couple dozen Belons on some Parisian terrace. Any man or woman worth their salt can open an oyster. Plus, standing around the kitchen shucking for a bunch of family and friends is way more fun than just putting an icy plate on the table. Oysters bring people together in a special way."

—Chris Sherman, Island Creek Oysters

DON'T MEAN TO PRY

Like the New England lobster, oysters are part of a long line of workingman's foods that have become a luxury. Due to their high protein-to-cost ratio, oysters were a popular and inexpensive food up until the beginning of the twentieth century. Their association as an aphrodisiac was born out of the myth that Aphrodite, the Greek goddess of love, sprang forth from the sea on an oyster shell. In fact, oysters are high in zinc, a deficiency of which can lead to impotence—though there is little scientific evidence for the fortifying fable of oysters increasing drive. Either way, oysters make a meal just a little more special once you know how to coax them out of their shells.

STABBER METHOD
Using an inflexible pointed knife (sometimes called a Chesapeake stabber knife), wedge the blade (with the edge facing away from you) between the two shells, roughly one-third up from the hinge, where the abductor is located. Gently twist the knife a few times until you feel a pop, then run the blade along the top shell and then the bottom to sever the abductor. Industrial shuckers use this method—along with a pair of puncture-proof gloves.

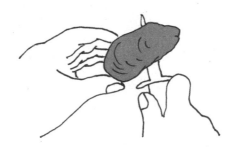

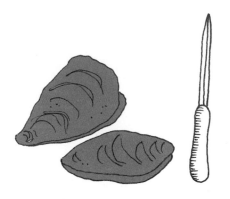

LOLLIPOP OR HINGE METHOD

Insert the knife into the hinge, gently wiggling the blade until you hear the hinge pop. With the blade inside, but the shell still sealed, scrape between the top of the shell and the oyster to cut the upper abductor muscle, then repeat for the bottom muscle. Style points for finishing with a Philly Flip, a trick move that flips the meat over (with the oyster cut free) to showcase the smoother side of the flesh in the "cup," or lower curved shell, while concealing any tears that may have occurred during opening. (Why Philly? The city had almost four hundred oyster houses by the late nineteenth century.) This maneuver also lets you check for shell flakes that might have fallen into the "liquor" (the liquid inside the shell) surrounding the shucked oyster.

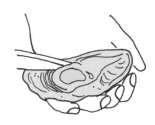

UNION OYSTER HOUSE METHOD

Insert your knife at the hinge and invert the oyster, with the knife butt pointing down to the table. Tap the butt on a stone or other sturdy surface until the blade point splits the hinge. Separate the two halves of the shell, releasing the oyster from its top shell but leaving it attached to the bottom shell, or cup, so the oyster is alive until served and slurped down. Wear thick gloves—the folks at Union Oyster House know what they're doing. (The Boston establishment has been open since 1827, making it the oldest continually operating restaurant in the United States.)

Shell It Out

What to do with all those shells? Crush them on your driveway for that Cape Cod look all year round, grind them up and feed to your chickens to strengthen their eggshells, or add the shells to your soil for extra calcium. Most areas reuse oyster shells to cultivate and restore oyster beds. Used shells can also be repurposed as a construction material called tabby, which is used in houses, patios, and sidewalks.

TOOL OF THE TRADE

Curved-Tip Oyster Knife

A common misconception is that the duller the oyster knife blade, the safer it is. In fact, a blunt tip requires extra force to get into the hinge, and that ends up being riskier than its sharper competition. You want a sturdy blade with a good point for plenty of leverage at the hinge, like this model, which has been handmade in New England since 1854 using only American materials.

SABER A CHAMPAGNE BOTTLE

—

"Champagne sabering adds a festive pop to any occasion. The technique is said to have been going since Napoleon Bonaparte's armies lopped the tops off champagne bottles to celebrate their victories. There's a bit of physics, a bit of danger, and, of course, a lot of confidence involved. The glimmer of the steel knife, the bubbles, and the light filtered through the glass bottle create quite the spectacle."

—Becky Sue Epstein, wine and spirits author

OFF WITH ITS HEAD!

Although sabering off the top of a champagne bottle might seem like a feat best left to a professional pirate, a few simple pointers will sharpen your technique considerably. When sabering—there are experts you can hire, if ever you start to feel weak wristed—do it outside where you have plenty of room, and practice with a cheap bottle beforehand. Because, as Napoleon would surely agree, the only thing worse than botching a sabering job is wasting good champagne.

1 Chill the champagne bottle by fully submerging it in an ice bucket (the neck also needs to be cold) or refrigerating it for two to four hours. The cold ensures that the glass is brittle and the liquid is as carbonated as possible. Chilled champagne will expel from the bottle as a controlled stream of foam when sabered, whereas sabering warm or room-temperature champagne will cause the bottle to explode.

2 Unpeel the foil of the chilled bottle and remove the wire cage so that the neck is completely exposed.

3 Find the crease, or the seam, where the two halves of the bottle meet. The bottle is weakest where this seam meets the lip; this is the place you will strike. Run your knife along the seam a few times to get your bearings without hitting the lip. (The saber itself doesn't break the bottle: it propagates a small crack that allows the pressure inside to release and the brittle glass to separate cleanly.)

→

4 In one hand, hold the body of the bottle (not the neck) pointing away from you at 45 degrees to the ground. Place the blade flat against the bottle, with the edge aimed toward the lip. Swiftly and surely glide the knife all the way along the seam and right through the lip with the force of slamming a door. This motion will take the top off the bottle. Make sure to keep your hands off the neck at all times; only the blade should be in contact.

5 Leave the bottle at 45 degrees for a few seconds, so that the pressure of the carbonated beverage pushes out any miniscule shards of glass in a foamy stream—and also for dramatic effect. Then bring your champagne flutes to the bottle and let the party begin!

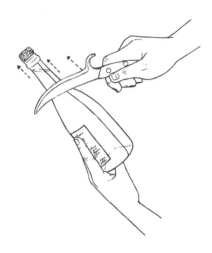

A Drop in Time

Champagne has a long history of fueling celebrations. Starting in the late fifth century, French kings held their coronations in the city of Reims, in the heart of the Champagne-Ardenne region. Festivities were held before and after the crowning, during which time the famed fizzy libation flowed freely. The sparkling beverage continued to whet the whistles of merrymakers during the Napoleonic Era, according to popular lore. In 1814, triumphant in the hard-won Battle of Reims, the thirsty and victorious French cavalry reputedly grabbed bottles of champagne and, from atop their horses, sliced off the tops with their sabers, spraying the effervescent liquid dramatically into the air. The saddled soldiers rode away while guzzling their bottles of champagne, leaving a trail of foam and dust in their wake.

Italian Stainless Steel Champagne Knife

Use a saber knife that is specifically made for opening champagne. You want something fairly well balanced, since you'll be holding the bottle in one hand and the saber in the other—nothing too long or unwieldy. This knife, made in Italy since 1912 by a family-run company, has an upswept, high-carbon, stainless steel blade and protective finger-hook handle.

MAKE
FIRE CIDER

"Nature is generous; its medicines, uncomplicated.
The hours and minutes spent carefully conjuring a remedy
with your own two hands, using only what the earth
offers freely, is an alchemical process of healing all its own.
To then be able to share the fruits of this labor and
bear witness to the growing health and vitality of those you
hold dear is surely one of life's greatest rewards."

—Sophia Rose, La Abeja Herbs

(EXTRA) HOT SHOT

Your first shot of fire cider goes something like this: Wince. Shake head. Swallow. You'll feel instantly fortified and wonder, What is this magical concoction? Traditionally a cold remedy and health tonic, fire cider has antiviral, anti-inflammatory, immune-boosting, decongestant, and digestive properties. Needless to say, all that strength means that this cure-all is not for sensitive palates or the lily livered. During cold and flu season, take a tablespoon a day as a preventative measure or 3 to 4 tablespoons at the first signs of sickness, repeating every three or four hours until symptoms subside.

The name *fire cider* hints at its ingredients: *fire* for horseradish and ginger roots, jalapeño peppers, and turmeric powder; *cider* for the apple cider vinegar base, which promotes extraction. Depending on what's in season, you can add orange rind or throw in fresh herbs, such as rosemary or thyme. Variations of the recipe abound, but here is our go-to. Whatever you choose to include in your mix, organic ingredients are always recommended.

INGREDIENTS

- 1 quart apple cider vinegar
- ½ cup fresh, grated ginger root
- ½ cup fresh, grated horseradish root
- 1 medium onion, chopped
- 10 cloves garlic, crushed or chopped
- 2 jalapeño peppers, chopped
- 1 lemon, juice and a bit of zest
- 1 tablespoon turmeric powder
- ¼ teaspoon cayenne powder
- 2 tablespoons dried rosemary leaves *or* several sprigs fresh rosemary
- ½ cup raw honey, or to taste

1. Prepare all the ingredients and combine them (except for the honey) in a quart-size jar. Place a piece of parchment or wax paper under the lid to prevent the corrosive vinegar from coming into contact with the metal.

2. Store the mixture in a dark, cool place for one month. Remember to shake daily. (According to folk-medicine traditions, the jar was buried underground to control temperature and promote further extraction. When solstice came around, the vessel was ceremoniously dug up and the fire cider enjoyed.)

3. After a month, pour the liquid into another clean jar. Strain the pulp through a cheesecloth, squeezing occasionally to ensure you get as much liquid out as possible.

4. Add ¼ cup raw honey and stir well, then mix in the remaining ¼ cup, or add honey to taste. The honey should only be mixed in at the time of consumption. Otherwise, its natural antibiotic properties could kill all the good bacteria you wanted to grow, and the natural sugars could also favor yeast rather than bacterial fermentation, creating a boozy cider.

5. To use your fire cider as a decongestant, simply add to a bowl of steaming water, place a towel over your head, and breathe deeply. There, all better.

PRESERVE
FRESH HERBS

—

"Oftentimes, a recipe calls for just one or two teaspoons
of fresh herbs, like basil or rosemary. But once you
mince up a few sprigs, you're still left with a significant amount
of herbs that need to be used—soon. Since I run a small
herb farm with my partner, I'm constantly inventing
new uses for them. Mix herbs into a basic olive oil and
balsamic vinaigrette to brighten up a salad. Add your dried
herbs to home-baked bread or dust them over a soft
cheese, such as fresh chèvre."

—Taylor Mardis Katz, Free Verse Farm

FIRST CUT, FIRST PRESERVED

Different types of herbs require different methods of preservation. Here are the top three.

WATER

When preserving herbs with a lot of water in them—such as chives, parsley, or cilantro—your best bet is to treat them like a bouquet of flowers: trim the stems, place them in a jar with water, and either store them on the counter (if you'll use them within a day or two) or in the refrigerator (if you want them to last a little longer). For the latter, remember to change the water every day.

Treat your herbs like a bouquet of flowers: trim the stems and place them in a jar with water.

OIL

To preserve your fresh herbs in oil, place a sprig or two of fresh rosemary, or any other hardy herb, in a tall, slender jar of olive oil. Keep in the refrigerator and use within four days for mixing into salad dressings or drizzling over roasted vegetables. Another option is to chop up your herbs and place them into an ice cube tray, topping up with olive oil until almost full and storing in the freezer. The oil reduces some of the browning and freezer burn, so you'll maintain the flavor when thawed.

AIR

If you're working with stalky varieties, such as thyme or oregano, the best method is drying. Spread the herbs on a dinner plate and place them on the stovetop for a day or two, with the oven and burners off. The radiant heat from the pilot light will dry the herbs at a nice, slow pace without singeing the delicate stalks. Remember to flip them once or twice a day so they dry evenly. (This method also works with the herbs inside your oven—just don't forget they're in there!) Once dried, strip the leaves off the stalks and store them in a small, airtight container in the cupboard, away from direct sunlight. You'll notice that the herbs you dry yourself are much greener and more flavorful than the ones you buy at the store.

Cut and Dry

Once you have a reserve of dried herbs, add them to anything that could benefit from extra flavor. Mix them into cream cheese, or roll a log of fresh chèvre over a bed of crumbled herbs on a dinner plate until it's fully coated. The most classic combination is herb butter—two ingredients that were made for each other. Here's how to make your own:

1 Leave a stick of butter out on your counter for half a day, allowing it to soften.

2 Place the butter in a small bowl and add your dried herbs, mixing until evenly distributed.

3 To preserve your herbed butter for later, cover a small saucer with a square of parchment paper. Scoop 2 to 4 tablespoons of the butter atop the paper, and mold it into a circle (the saucer acts as your shaping mechanism). Cover the butter with another piece of parchment and fold up the edges, securing them with tape or string.

4 Store the discs in a small, airtight container in the freezer.

You can thaw the amount you need at the drop of a hat, impressing any friends who happen to stop by.

CARE FOR KITCHEN KNIVES

—

"Cooking is an art and a craft. Like any craftsman,
you must maintain your tools. Buy a quality knife (you really
don't need more than three) and appreciate the food
that it makes possible to cook and eat. Love it. Pay attention
to it. Treat it as a member of the family. If you do,
cooking and preparation will be a true pleasure. Nothing
beats the sheer joy of a taking a whole bag of
onions and cutting them into a pile of paper-thin slices."

—Tom Mylan, butcher and author

KEEP YOUR EDGE

There is wisdom in the chef's maxim, "Your knife is an extension of yourself." Depending on the job at hand, a properly chosen knife will effortlessly cut a T-bone steak, crack through a coconut, or delicately slice pillowy-soft white bread.

HONING

Every time you cut through a piece of food, minute metal burrs and microscopic bits of food dull your knife's sharpness. Ideally, you should hone it after every use. Many knife sets come with a long tubular steel rod—this is your knife steel (often wrongly referred to as a knife sharpener).

1 Fix the steel rod in one hand or on a counter top, pointing away from you.
2 Place the heel of the knife (the end nearest to the handle) against the tip of the steel rod and slowly glide the knife down, maintaining a 22-degree angle along the entire length of the blade. At the end of this motion, the whole blade should have touched the steel.
3 Repeat about eight to ten times on both sides.
4 Wipe off the metal particles with a clean, soft towel.

SHARPENING

A dull blade will bruise ingredients; a sharp blade will make precise and efficient cuts. (An easy way to test sharpness is to see if your knife can easily cut through a sheet of paper.) To give you a sense of how frequently you should sharpen your knives, daily cooks sharpen their knives once or twice a year.

1 Place the whetstone, with the coarse grit facing up, on a secure, nonslippery surface.
2 Using one hand, grasp the knife by the handle and hold the cutting edge, facing away from you, against the stone, tip first, at 22 degrees.
3 Applying pressure, slide the blade forward and across the whetstone, covering the entire length of the blade and keeping it against the stone at a constant 22 degrees.
4 Repeat about ten times for each side of the blade.
5 Flip the stone over to the fine-grit surface and give each side of the blade about ten strokes, just as you did before.
6 Use your knife steel to hone the blade, then rinse and wipe it dry to remove any metal particles.

Cooking is an art and a craft. Like any craftsman, you must maintain your tools.

The Kindest Cut

No matter what type of knife you're using, here are the universal dos and don'ts when cutting:

- Cut only on wood, bamboo, or plastic surfaces. The impact of materials such as glass, granite, or porcelain will damage the blade.

- If possible, use a rocking or sliding motion when cutting. Avoid chopping, as the impact will dull the blade.

- Use the spine of the blade and not the sharp edge to transfer ingredients from your cutting surface.

MAKE
RED WINE
VINEGAR

—

"Red wine vinegar is one of the cornerstones of vinaigrettes, but it can also spark up sauces or make a tenderizing marinade. When I first started making my own red wine vinegar, I set up a blind tasting with my wife: my first batch versus the hodgepodge of vinegars we had on our pantry shelf. Mine had a rich, ruby-red color and sharp flavor. The others were wan in comparison. I've never bought wine vinegar since. As far as food preservation goes, vinegar is one of the least labor-intensive and most rewarding projects."

—Derrick Schneider, food writer and experimenter

FIND YOUR MOTHER AND DO THE MATH

Vinegar making is basic science. In the presence of oxygen, *Acetobacter* bacteria in red wine feed off the alcohol and convert it into acetic acid. That acid, plus the water from the wine, creates vinegar. In theory, an open bottle of wine left on a counter could produce vinegar. In practice, this rarely works (wine makers try to prevent this from happening, after all). Give yourself a hand by using an existing culture, called a mother, and adding wine to that. You can find a mother by asking a vinegar-making friend, or buy it from a wine or brewing retailer, such as oakbarrel.com. Just remember that commercial vinegar is often pasteurized, killing off bacteria and therefore making it unsuitable as a mother.

GETTING STARTED

Once you've found a mother, you can add post-party dregs or buy $10 table wines. (Red wine generally has fewer sulfites, which slow down vinegar production, than white wine.) The bacteria need oxygen, but that's easy to get. Leave your vinegar container—a large glass jar if you don't want to splurge on a barrel—open to the air, covering any openings with cheesecloth to keep the flies out. Periodically (once a day when you're motivated, once a week when you're less so) whisk the vinegar into a frenzy to give the culture a bit of a rush. This significantly increases the surface area of oxygen in the liquid. If whisked continuously, the wine could produce vinegar in just a day!

FOOD FOR THOUGHT

Acetobacter also need food. Though they'll happily chomp away at alcohol, too much will kill them. Tolerance varies by species, but try to never exceed 10 percent alcohol by volume. The math on this is easy: Round your alcohol percentage up to the next number, just to be safe. Multiply that number by 10, then subtract 100. This final number is the percentage of water relative to the volume of wine you need to add to your wine before adding it to the vinegar. For example, 14.5 percent wine rounds up to 15 percent. Fifteen times 10 equals 150. One hundred subtracted from 150 equals 50. So, in order to dilute 750 ml of wine with an alcohol percentage of 14.5 percent down to 10 percent alcohol by volume, you need to add about 375 ml of water to the wine. No need to get out the graduated cylinders. Just eyeball in a measuring cup and err on the side of more water. Note that there's a 1:1 correspondence between the alcohol level and the level of acidity. A 10 percent wine, for example, will produce a much stronger vinegar. In other words, don't blindly add whatever a recipe calls for. Add to taste.

FINISHING TOUCHES

How do you know it's ready? Smell your batches regularly, and when the scent is more akin to vinegar than nail polish remover, consider them done. Six weeks or so is usually enough, though the process sometimes takes up to two months. Leave about one-third of the batch in the container and add more wine to start the process again. Every vinegar maker treats their stash differently. Some people bottle theirs. Some filter or pasteurize it. We strain ours through cheese-cloth into bottles, then leave them in a cool spot for six months to mellow.

The Many Uses of Vinegar

Vin aigre (roughly translated from French as "sour wine") is the result of the slow decay of everything from grapes to beets, malts to grains, apples to honey, each producing distinctive vinegars. Kimchi, sauerkraut, and kosher dill pickles are only a few of the tasty vinegar-preserved treats from around the globe. Versatile as it is as a foodstuff, vinegar's usefulness doesn't stop there. The acids in apple cider vinegar make it a natural healing remedy and particularly suited to detoxifying. Those same acidic properties also make vinegar efficient for natural household cleaning, dissolving soap scum and stains, and, combined with baking soda, unclogging drains.

During the Black Death, thieves used vinegar to protect themselves from germs as they stole from the dead. During the Civil War, vinegar was an antibiotic used to heal wounds. Roman legionnaires drank vinegar before going into battle. Sailors preserved foods for long voyages and swabbed their decks with a splash of vinegar. Cleopatra, after betting she could "consume a fortune in a single meal," dissolved a pearl in a glass of vinegar and drank it—proving the true value of this acidic elixir.

BREW
COFFEE

—

"I love the challenge of sourcing, roasting, brewing, and, finally, tasting exceptional coffee. The most important thing to keep in mind is the quality of the raw product. Try to buy from roasters who uphold transparency and traceability. I always recommend asking your local barista or coffee roaster to suggest two coffees with very different flavor profiles. Then compare and contrast, and practice tasting the subtleties between the two. It's amazing how quickly you can develop your palate."

—Lance Schnorenberg, Lofted Coffee Roasters

THE BEST PART OF WAKING UP

The smell of coffee alone perks up a groggy mind. While caffeine is the most effective ingredient for giving you a boost of energy and mental clarity, there's something meditative about brewing coffee every morning. Those fifteen or so minutes offer a quiet routine to savor before the rush of a normal day begins.

Below are two of the most common coffee-making methods: the pour-over and the cold brew.

THE POUR-OVER

The pour-over gives you greater control when you're brewing coffee in small batches. It's the perfect way to make one or two cups that come out full and flavorful. There are multiple pour-over coffeemakers, including the Hario v60 (for the experienced barista), the Chemex (for making several cups at a time), the Kone (to avoid using filters), and the Walkure (for the modern design geek). The brewing steps are all very similar regardless of the vessel you choose. These instructions, however, are specific to a ceramic coffee dripper.

1 The amount of coffee you use depends on how much coffee you want to brew and how dark you like it. For a medium roast that makes 1 to 2 cups, start with 4 tablespoons of beans.

2 Grind the beans to a medium-coarse grind, roughly the texture of sea salt.

3 Place a no. 2 or no. 4 filter in the dripper and wet the inner walls with hot water. This does two things: First, it removes loose dust and filter particles. Second, it warms up the inside of the dripper to help keep a consistent temperature when brewing.

4 Pour the grounds into the filter and place the dripper on top of a cup or pitcher that will catch the brewed coffee.

5 Bring a kettle of water to a boil, pull off the heat, and let the bubbling settle, around thirty seconds.

6 Set a timer to three minutes. (Brewing past three minutes can result in bitter coffee.) Then pour a small amount of water onto the grounds (just enough to soak the beans), keeping the spout close to the surface to decrease agitation and maintain temperature. Allow thirty seconds for the beans to expand, or "bloom."

7 Repeat the process, pouring quickly, gently, and evenly in a circular motion. Pause between each pour while the water drips through.

8 Once the timer goes off, remove the dripper from the pitcher or mug and enjoy.

THE COLD BREW

Cold-brew coffee uses cold- or room-temperature water to extract flavor. The process creates a syrupy coffee that's low in acidity—great for people with sensitive stomachs. For a proper cold brew, you need to allow twelve to twenty-four hours of brewing time. The most popular method is known as the Toddy Cold Brew System, created in 1964 by the chemical engineer Todd Smith. But there are several easier ways to make cold brew, including using a French press, as outlined here.

1 Again, the amount of beans you use is dependent on the size of your French press and how much coffee you want to make. We recommend a 3:1 ratio, meaning for every three cups of water, use one cup of beans.

2 Grind your beans extra coarse and add to the French press.

3 Pour cold water over the grounds.

4 Use a wooden spoon to stir the grounds, ensuring that they are all wet. The mixture should be thick, like wet cement.

5 Before refrigerating, place the lid of the French press over the grounds, but don't press down on the plunger.

6 After twelve to twenty-four hours, remove the press from the fridge and press the plunger all the way down to filter out the grounds. Transfer the cold brew into a separate serving pitcher and enjoy. You can add ice or hot water (using a 1:1 ratio with the cold brew) for a balanced and flavorful iced or hot coffee.

Chemex Coffeemaker

This elegant vessel first appeared in 1941 as the invention of an expat
German scientist named Peter J. Schlumbohm, who was on the hunt for a decent
cup of coffee in New York, dissatisfied with the bitter offerings from
automats and late-night diners. The result was a thermal carafe drip system
made from high-quality borosilicate glass. To test out your Chemex,
follow the pour-over instructions, using a medium-to-coarse grind and
a Chemex filter.

SHAKE
A COCKTAIL

—

"Spirits, bitters, and sugar are the trinity of basic cocktail ingredients, along with water as a result of the ice melting. An old-fashioned is therefore the quintessential cocktail, hitting all three ingredients, and thought by many to be the oldest cocktail in existence (hence the name). Since there are so few ingredients in an old-fashioned, preparation is key. No surprise, then, that asking a bartender to make one is akin to asking a chef to cook an egg: a deceptively simple undertaking that requires real skill."

—Brandon Davey, bartender

CREATE A STIR, SHAKE IT UP

First, prepare your glassware, whether adding ice to the glass or chilling it in the refrigerator. (If it's a coupe, fill it with ice so the glass is cool but the stem remains at room temperature, so as to not freeze the sipper's fingers.)

Next, build up your drink station. Use two stainless steel shakers of different sizes—not glass, which is inflexible and therefore more susceptible to breakage when you're trying to pop the two pieces apart. Place the smaller shaker closer to you on the bar and the larger shaker behind it. Add all of your ingredients to the smaller shaker, starting with the least expensive. (If you mess up ratios and need to start again, you're tossing simple syrup rather than a ten-year-old Scotch). When you're ready to shake, add ice into the bigger shaker. This allows you to better see and smell your mix.

THE SHAKE

Tap the tins together once to secure them in place, always keeping the larger tin on the bottom. With one hand, place two fingers on either side of the seam where the tins meet, like you would a football. Beginners can place the other hand on the bottom shaker for added support.

The goal is to impart as much cold as possible. You want to "wake up" the cocktail so that it's cloudy when poured. Shake hard and short, rather than long and soft, for roughly twenty seconds, holding the shakers either in front of you or up by your ear.

Tap at the seam with the palm of your hand to separate the two shakers. Empty the ice from the cup, or retrieve a chilled cup from the fridge, but leave the shakers closed, and don't open them until you're ready to pour.

THE POUR

The average cocktail starts with 3 ½ to 4 ounces of liquid and should finish with 5 ½ to 6 ounces from the water dilution, creating the ideal balance.

For an extra smooth beverage, double strain your cocktail using a Hawthorne strainer, which features a spring that tightens around the lip of the shaker and lets in less ice, followed by a Chinois filter (or any small mesh strainer will do the trick). This way you avoid the layer of ice "crème" that forms on the surface—although some bartenders, like many in Japan, leave the crème for that extra bit of froth. For stirred cocktails, go with a julep strainer.

THE STIR

As a general rule of thumb, shake drinks if fruit or citrus juice is involved; stir if your cocktail has only spirits. Shaking incorporates air, creating a frothiness that's pleasant on the tongue. A martini, however, should be smooth, unclouded, and… stirred.

Stir your spirit as vigorously as you can, but don't impart air bubbles. This gentler process takes twice as long as shaking to fully dilute the ice. Aim for around forty seconds if using regular ice that isn't shaved or crushed, which melt faster.

THE GARNISH

Much of a well-made drink is simply the aroma. Add a nice slice of lemon or orange zest cut with a peeler, or a knife for a more substantial piece. The garnish—a few sprigs of fresh mint, for example, or even an edible flower, such as violet or lavender—builds on the sensory experience of a carefully crafted cocktail. The same idea applies to the rim: a kick of pepper in a salt rim or a hint of cinnamon in a sugar rim enhances the flavor of your drink.

Keep Your Cool

Normally, when you fill an ice tray, the cubes freeze from the outside in, pushing air to the center. But if you pack your tray with crushed ice and top it off with a splash of water, the cubes will freeze from the inside out, creating a solid block without the usual oxygen bubble. A regular bag of ice from the corner store is all you need. Give it a few good smacks on the counter or ground to crush up any big chunks, then start filling your tray. Use filtered water for topping off, since chlorinated water will affect the flavor of your drink. You can also make one big block of ice in a big freezer-friendly container and chip away at it when cocktail hour rolls around.

TOOL OF THE TRADE

Italian Pewter Jigger

To jig or not to jig? Each brand of speed pour is different. Plus, the viscosity of your liquor varies: a sugary rum flows slower than a gin, for example. A jigger saves you time—especially one that is double-sided, allowing you to measure half an ounce or one and a half ounces with the flip of a wrist. Hand cast in northern Italy, this jigger is made from pewter, a low-maintenance material that builds up an attractive patina over time.

FRY, SCRAMBLE, AND POACH AN EGG

—

"The humble egg makes the perfect comfort meal, whether starting your day or fueling a late night. It's a building block that can serve as both garnish and main course—not to mention that it's quick to prepare, affordable, and one of the few fresh, nutritious things you can pick up at almost any corner store. A young chef's skill set can be assessed by how well he or she can prepare a 'simple' egg. Once you've mastered the technique, enjoy your eggs with a few slices of smoked salmon and crunchy sea salt, or on buttered sourdough toast with crisped sage leaves, or on a bed of spinach with shaved parmesan and olive oil."

—Jody Williams, Buvette Gastrothèque

GOOD EGGS

Know your eggs. Ideally, they're organic and come from a nearby farm. When cracked into the frying pan, fresh egg whites will be viscous and form that iconic round shape without the need for a mold. The yolk will sit proudly on top of the whites. If your egg white runs all over the pan, it's less fresh. Good eggs come in all different sizes and colors, unlike the more uniform industrial versions that can be purchased in standard sizes. Also, if you happen upon a double yolk, it's said to be good luck.

FRY

Your pan should be just big enough to hold the number of eggs you plan to cook, but make no more than four at a time. Any more and things will start to get unwieldy.

Add your fat (olive oil, bacon fat, butter, etc.) into the pan before turning on the heat so you can adjust the temperature as needed and better prevent the fat from burning. Set the heat to medium-low and wait until the fat begins to foam and sizzle. Your mouth should now be watering.

To avoid shells, crack your egg into a ramekin *before* pouring it into the pan. For sunny-side up, let the egg whites turn opaque and cover the pan, keeping the heat at medium-low for another three minutes. Drop in a sage leaf toward the end to soak up a bit of fat. Scoop up the egg and serve.

SCRAMBLE

Crack three eggs into a bowl and start whisking with a fork. Add crème fraîche, fresh herbs, or any other ingredients you see fit.

Use a small pan with higher edges, roughly two inches tall. Add butter and set the heat to medium. Wait for that soft sizzling to begin, then pour your egg mix into the pan and grab your trustiest wooden spoon. Keep stirring, keep stirring, keep stirring— much like you would a risotto. Scrape the bottom after every few strokes. Once the eggs start to form small curds and the mixture is cooked but still loose enough to pour, remove your pan from the heat and stir in a little (or a lot) more butter. The residual heat will continue to cook the eggs until they are ready to serve. Look for a creamy texture, unless you like them firm.

POACH

You can use the same high-edged pan as you did for the scrambled eggs, or use a tall pot of around eight inches or more in height. (The greater depth cooks the eggs more evenly.)

Fill your vessel with water until about three-quarters full, or enough to fully submerge the eggs, and add a good pinch of salt and a teaspoon of white vinegar (which is not for flavor alone but also to give the eggs form). Crack your eggs into individual ramekins.

When the water reaches a steady simmer, stir it in a clockwise motion so the whites will wrap around the yolks. Gently slide in the eggs one by one at ten-second intervals. You can also use a slotted spoon, which strains off the thinner whites for a more compact poached egg.

Wait for the whites to set and cook through, making sure the water remains at a nice, even simmer. This should take around three minutes, after which you can scoop up the eggs with the slotted spoon, strain well, and enjoy immediately.

Make a Clean Break

To crack an egg efficiently, hold the egg with one hand and tap it firmly (one time only!) against the side of your bowl or pan. This should create a clean break—multiple taps will result in fragmented shells. To separate the egg whites from the yolk, crack the egg over a bowl, part the shell enough for the whites to run out, then pass the yolk from shell to shell, letting the rest of the whites run out into the bowl.

TOOL OF THE TRADE

English Terra-Cotta Egg Rack

Many cooks prefer to create their dishes using eggs that have been stored at room temperature rather than refrigerated, as the eggs tend to react more quickly, rise more easily, and incorporate better with other ingredients. (Think higher cakes with a tender crumb that bake up in a jiffy.) This egg rack is made in England using terra-cotta. The cool, porous ceramic helps the eggs safely and slowly reach room temperature without sweating, which can promote bacteria.

PICKLE AND PRESERVE

—

"The act of food preservation, for me, is a celebration of each
season and the mindfulness it takes to eat good tomatoes
with a clear conscience in February. It's a response to our current
thoughtless, cheap food culture. Preserving your food
takes time and a little work, but there's nothing more satisfying
or impressive than making a soup or stew from vegetables
you preserved on a summer night, or slathering
your morning waffles with apple butter you toiled over
a few months earlier."

—Kelly Geary, *Sweet Deliverance*

YES, YOU CAN

Once essential methods of making fruits and veggies close to imperishable during endless stretches of cold and frozen earth, pickling and preservation have evolved into artful ways of capturing the vibrant flavors of the seasons, placing them under glass in a kind of butterfly collection of beautiful flavors to enjoy any time of the year. Pickling and preserving employ the help of Mother Nature's own natural fermentation skills, and while both processes may seem simple, there's a chance for mold or other harmful bacteria or pathogens to make their way into your pickle and jam jars. Be extra diligent in handling each step with care and cleanliness. The basic idea is that you want to keep in all the good bacteria while sealing out the bad stuff. If you doubt the safety of anything you make at home, do not eat it.

Regardless of what kind of pickle you're making, start with the freshest ingredients. The point is to preserve your bounty's flavor at its finest. Discard the soft, the wilted, the limp. Then roll up your sleeves and get started.

TO SALT OR TO VINEGAR?

Pickling can be done utilizing one of two methods—with salt as the primary instigator of fermentation or with vinegar, which is a quicker process. If you choose to use vinegar, your flavors will vary depending on the type, from the delicate hint of rice vinegar to the bracing rush of apple cider vinegar. On the other hand, the salt-brine method offers up flavor, clean and simple, allowing the personality of the pickled veggie or fruit to dominate.

BASIC PICKLING WITH VINEGAR

Rather than fermenting, pickles in a vinegar solution settle in for long-term preservation. The acetic acid in vinegar makes this an ideal method to create an environment where no nasty microorganisms can thrive.

Sterilize Your Instruments

Use clean towels, rinse your utensils with boiling water, and boil your jars for a few minutes before starting. The lids should be rinsed in warm water.

Gather Your Ingredients

Wash and trim your veggies—be it the classic cucumber or something more daring, like purple cauliflower or pearl onions—so that they will fit nicely when placed lengthwise into your jar. Thickness may vary from ½ to 1 ½ inches, depending on the vegetable—any thicker and it may not pickle completely. The harder the produce, the longer it will take to pickle; the more porous, the quicker. Choose your salt, preferably of the pickling, canning, or kosher variety. (Iodized salt will cloud pickling water and doesn't impart as much flavor.) You'll also need any spices, herbs, or other tasty ingredients you want to throw in.

Make Your Pickle Brine

The following are the basic pickle proportions. Use more or less, depending on your needs and taste.

4	pounds any vegetables
2 ¾	cups vinegar (apple cider, rice, white, or red wine)
3	cups water
¼	cup salt

Mix the salt, vinegar, and water in a regular saucepan on medium heat, stirring until the salt dissolves, and bring to a boil.

Pack Your Jars

Add your selected herbs and spices to the bottom of each jar, saving a bit extra for topping up at the end. Ensure that your jar is still hot—not room temperature, since this could cause the glass to crack when coming in contact with the just-boiled pickle juice. Add your veggies, packing them in tightly. Pour in the hot pickle juice, leaving at least ½ inch of space at the top of the jar. Throw in the remaining herbs and spices. Clean the rim of the jar with a clean, damp cloth to ensure proper seal, and screw on the lid securely with a kitchen towel.

Seal the Deal

Carefully place your sealed jars in a sturdy stockpot with at least one inch of water covering the lids. Bring to a boil for seven to ten minutes. (Add five minutes for every 1,000 feet above sea level, depending on where you live.) When in doubt, it's better to round up estimates, since the longer you boil your jars, the more bacteria you're killing. Using tongs and keeping safely away from the hot water, pull out the jars and set them aside to cool. You'll hear the lids pop from the air compression—the sound of all that pickle goodness being properly sealed in. Once cool, tap the jars gently on your countertop to remove any air bubbles.

Now Wait

From here on in, let the veggies do the work. The longer they sit, the more pickled they will become. Vinegar pickles can last up to two years in the pantry.

BASIC PICKLING WITH SALT

Lacto-fermentation is a traditional method of making pickles without vinegar. Plus, you keep all the "good for you" bacteria. Pickling with salt follows the same basic instructions as the vinegar-based method, with a few key differences (the brine and packing). There is no need to seal your jars in boiling water. The holy triumvirate of water, salt, and veggie—used in all great lacto-fermented recipes, from German sauerkraut to Korean kimchi—works its magic.

Make Your Brine

For every 1 quart of water, add about 1 ½ tablespoons of salt (kosher, sea or pickling but not iodized). With this ratio, use approximately 3 pounds of veggies. Combine water and salt in a large jar or bottle (a clean wine bottle works just fine) and shake well to ensure that all the salt has dissolved.

Pack Your Jars

Add your selected spices to the bottom of the jars. Pack in your veggies, and then pour in the brine, leaving at least ½ inch of space at the top of the jar. Screw the lid on tight. Leave the jars in a cool place and wait about a week before tasting. Continue pickling until desired taste is reached, then keep your jars in the fridge. Whereas vinegar pickles can last for a year in the fridge, salt pickles will only last about a month.

SMALL-BATCH JAM MAKING

There are two ways of approaching jam and jelly making. One is to use the traditional hot-water-bath canning technique for longer-lasting, large-batch jamming. The other is to make jams in small batches that you can eat and enjoy quickly before they spoil, which is what is outlined below, so you can taste the delicious fruits of your labor without delay.

Sterilize Your Instruments

Use clean towels, rinse your utensils with boiling water, and boil your jars for a few minutes before starting. The lids should be rinsed in warm water.

Gather Your Ingredients

Select the fruit of your choice (fresh picked is always best) with enough to make about 2 ½ cups once smashed or diced. Here's everything you'll need:

2 ½ cups fruit: smashed, diced, or sliced
1 lemon
¼ cup of sugar (or honey or agave), or to taste
natural pectin
a pinch of salt, or to taste
Note: *You can omit the pectin. Your jam will just be a bit runnier.*

Start Your Jam Session

Cut your fruit, discarding any pits, cores, or heavily bruised sections. Feel free to mash, chop, or slice, depending on the consistency of fruit you want in your final jam. Combine the fruit and sugar in a medium-size saucepan. If desired, add the pectin according to package directions. Sprinkle in a bit of salt to make the fruit flavor really pop and squeeze in some lemon to cut the sweetness until you find just the right balance between tart and sweet.

Test the Results

Bring the mixture to a boil. The moisture in the fruit will keep it from burning, but be sure to stir frequently so it doesn't stick to the pot. After about five to seven minutes of boiling, check to see if the jam is set, using this trusty trick to test your concoction: Put a few drops of jam on a frozen spoon. Wait a few seconds and then run your finger through the jam. If a trail appears on the spoon, the jam is done. If not, keep on cooking. You can also taste the jam at this point to see if it needs more sugar, more lemon, etc.

Set

Turn off the stove and carefully spoon the jam into jars. Set the jars aside to cool to room temperature. Then put on the lids, stick the jars in the fridge, and enjoy your jam for up to three weeks after opening.

Weck Canning Jars

When not holding and serving your jams, these glass jars do double duty
for canning asparagus, carrots, leeks, and other vegetables or fruit.
In 1900, the designer Johann Weck first released his jars, made with thick glass
to withstand boiling, sterilizing, and processing. The glass lids never rust or
contaminate the flavor of the food, and the tab on the replaceable rubber rings,
when facing downward, indicates clearly that the seal on that jar is intact.

TWO

Outdoors

HOW TO

—

SPLIT
WOOD

—

"I learned to split wood thanks to a father who insisted
that a young girl should grow up knowing how to do manual
labor. A person is not just born loving (and yearning!)
to mutilate logs—they have to learn. My first experience was
awful: the backbreaking struggle to remove my axe
from the stump in which I had naively embedded it, the
frustration of breaking the axe handle as I twisted and pulled.
In the end, I threw up my hands and stormed off, cussing.
Now I love splitting wood. It sharpens the mind and
is one of the most meditative, satisfying activities one could
ever undertake."

—Cass Daubenspeck, writer

A WOOD PRIMER

When splitting wood, you're not sawing or cutting but *smacking* the wood so that it splits open. (This is why people say a dull splitter works better than a sharp one.) Unlike the sharp, square blade of an axe, better for chopping down a tree or cutting thin branches, the wedge of a maul is designed to exert outward pressure on the wood for an easier split with fewer swings. Before beginning, check the round or log for any advantageous splits or cracks. Avoid hitting knots— those gnarled sections in the wood where the grain runs irregularly— as they're hard to break apart and will sap your energy, when they can simply be avoided. Keep in mind that the best blow will always be delivered near the edge of the round, not at the center. The growth rings closer to the bark of the tree are wider and more vulnerable, and easier to work apart. Here are a few more pointers.

SWING LIKE YOU MEAN IT
Stand with your feet shoulder width apart, elbows and knees comfortably bent. Hold the maul horizontally in front of you, at waist level. Grasp the neck of the handle with one hand and the butt of the handle with the other. Raise the maul high above your head until it's in line with the rest of your body, straightening your back and knees. During this upswing, slide the hand on the neck down to meet the hand holding the butt of the handle. Then begin a forceful downswing in one smooth movement, bending at the waist and knees. You'll most likely need to take a few swings before the wood splits. Just keep aiming for the split you're steadily creating.

FIND YOUR TARGET

Always lock your eyes on the spot you want the maul to hit, and don't take them off the target as you bring the blade down. As in karate or bowling, you have to visualize the follow-through.

REST UP

Splitting wood can be backbreaking work, and there's nothing more wasteful than slamming down the maul with less than your full strength. Rest between swings. If you feel tired, winded, or weak but continue to swing, your grip will change and compromise the process. Better to put the maul down and hit the same spot again when you're ready. Coincidentally, this applies to a lot of things in life.

As in karate or
*   bowling, you have*
to visualize
*   the follow-through.*

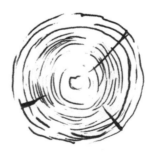

The Woodpile

It doesn't matter a whit what kind of wood you split and burn unless it's seasoned. Like a fine wine left to age, a piece of wood, depending on the type, has to sit for six months or more before it will burn hot and clean. Oak? A year at least! As for the woodpile, pick a dry location to stack it, such as a cement-floored patio with a roof. The cement keeps the bottom layer of wood from growing mold, and the roof provides shelter from rain and snow.

If you stack your wood in the yard, build a foundation layer of already-rotting wood you can sacrifice. Make sure it's kept where air and sun can dry it thoroughly and with the appropriate covering (a good tarp will do). Stack your wood in cords. (A cord is an area of stacked wood measuring 4 × 4 × 8 feet.)

START
A CAMPFIRE

—

"Now, as when I was a child, campfires lure me to
their edge. With the expected crackle and unexpected pop,
its warm face conjures up memories of the best joke
ever told, the unmistakable aroma of a meal being cooked
over an open flame, or simply a thoughtful look
exchanged in the dark. The campfire is an invitation.
It invites us to share with the community
that encircles its glow and to connect with the earth."

—Keith Hobbs, Idaho Department of Parks and Recreation

SET A SPARK

Evidence suggests that humans have been making fires for more than 1.2 million years, but practice still makes perfect. Here's a refresher on starting, maintaining, and putting out your fire.

1 Start the fire in a safe place, whether it's a concrete or stone fire ring that has been provided at a campsite or a beach, or a small hole encircled with rocks that's at least 5 feet from anything flammable, including your tent, belongings, and surrounding trees and foliage.

2 Gather the three types of materials you'll need:
   - *Tinder*: anything that will ignite easily, such as small twigs, dry leaves, newspaper, cardboard, or even dryer lint.
   - *Kindling*: small sticks and thin branches measuring about ½ inch in diameter and tree bark that is dry and will quickly catch fire.
   - *Firewood*: pieces 1 to 5 inches in diameter, as dry as possible.

3 Arrange your kindling in one of the following four configurations, according to none other than Smokey the Bear:
   - Lay your kindling in the shape of a tent or tipi over a handful of tinder. The upside-down-cone shape creates plenty of airflow to start and maintain a flame.
   - Place the kindling over the tinder in the shape of a cross for a long-burning fire.
   - For an even longer burn, stack your kindling at right angles, as if you are building a cabin out of Lincoln Logs, with the smallest pieces on top.
   - The lean-to configuration is especially suited for cooking. Drive a long kindling stick over a compact pile of tinder at a 30-degree angle into the ground, with the free end of the stick facing the direction of the wind. Lean the smaller pieces of kindling against either side of the angled stick, like a rib cage.

4 Add the firewood either before or after lighting the tinder and kindling, mirroring the method in which you laid the kindling. Once you have everything ready, ignite the tinder with a match, lighter, or magnesium fire starter. As the fire grows, add more tinder and blow lightly at its base to encourage the tinder and kindling to catch flame. Once they ignite, begin adding firewood if you haven't already.

A Note on Protocol
Always check on specific tips and rules and obtain necessary permits from the park where you will be camping and creating fires. National, state, and privately run parks all have their own guidelines for the protection of the land and its ecosystem.

Keep the Fires Burning

A fire requires three elements: dry wood, adequate airflow, and continuous heat. When adding more firewood, place the new logs down gently. Tossing them may create dangerous sparks and light an unwanted fire elsewhere. A carelessly pitched log could also cause shifts and collapses in the overall balance, causing the fire to either flare up or die right down. To encourage the fire, blow gently on the embers from the side, never from above, to protect your face.

Where There's Smoke. . . .

Add your last log about one hour before you want to extinguish the campfire, allowing time for it to burn out completely. Pour enough water on the burned-out fire to drown all the embers. Stir the ashes and the embers to ensure that the fire is completely extinguished. The ground should be cool to the touch.

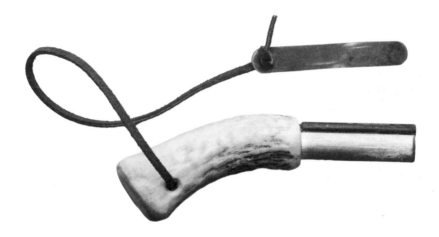

Elk-Antler Magnesium Fire Starter

Magnesium must be finely shaved to become flammable. Once burning, the shavings are hotter than a match, difficult to extinguish, and capable of lighting even damp kindling—good news for the cold camper stranded with a set of wet matches. Start by pressing the magnesium rod against a hard surface (the ground or a log) and use firm, even strokes with the steel striker, running the length of the rod, to create a small pile of shavings. Next, gather your kindling around the shavings. With a series of sharp strokes along the flint embedded in the rod, use the striker to set off sparks.

MASTER
BASIC KNOTS

—

"A knot is a continuous strand of rope that is altered and reconfigured to serve a new purpose and function. As sailors, journeyers, and tradesmen will attest, you must first understand the function of a knot before you can know how to use it. The moment a new group of passengers sets foot on my boat, I teach them how to tie a few useful knots. They gain a deepened appreciation for the importance of each knot. Plus, learning to correctly tie the right knot for the right job is incredibly satisfying."

—Dayyan Armstrong, Sailing Collective

CORD CURRICULUM

The measure of a good knot is not necessarily how easy it is to tie but rather how easy it is to *untie*. (Cue memory reel of someone secretly knotting your shoelaces together.) From the essential to the ornamental, knots have helped sailors and cowboys alike in getting out of (or into) a bind. So whether you're securing a boat to the dock or lashing flea-market finds to the roof of your car, here are a few essentials. (Note: avoid any rope that's frayed, damaged from excessive heat or sun, or has been stored in such a damp and dark place that it's molded.)

TONGUE-TIED?

Before you get started, some key terminology: the long end of the line that's not knotted is called the "standing end"; the end of the line that you use to create a knot is the "working end."

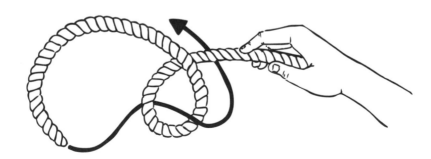

THE BOWLINE

Strong and easy to tie, the bowline (pronounced "bo-lin") is one of the most popular knots out there. It has endless uses, from attaching a line to a sail to tying down an aircraft during a windstorm, as the Federal Aviation Administration recommends. Because of its design, the bowline stays tied but can easily be undone, even on the frozen deck of a ship in the North Atlantic.

1 Hold the line in one hand, letting it hang down. With your other hand, make a small loop with the working end by folding the line over (never under) itself.
2 Pass the working end under and through the loop.
3 Wrap the line counterclockwise around the standing end and pass the working end down through the loop again.
4 Tighten the knot by pulling on the working end.

THE FIGURE EIGHT

This knot has two specific purposes. It can be used to form a strong loop but is also commonly used as a stopper knot to jam a loose line. For sailors, that means tying the figure eight at the end of a sheet so it won't run through a block and flap dangerously in the wind. For climbers, the figure eight is tied in the rope, and then the end is fed through a harness and led back through the figure eight, creating a double figure eight—a.k.a. a super-strong knot.

1 Hold the line in one hand. With your other hand, pass the line over and counterclockwise around itself.
2 Pass the working end through the loop you've created, and pull tight until you form an "8."

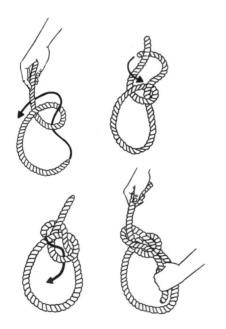

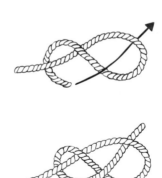

THE CLOVE HITCH

Hitches range from pretty basic (to tie your horse to a post) to more advanced (to tie a very big ship to a dock). The trucker's hitch, for example, comes in handy for everything from stretching your tent fly tight to securing your canoe to a car roof. The clove hitch, though not the strongest binding knot, allows for some adjustment even after it has been tied, making it useful in a variety of situations.

1 Loop the working end clockwise around a vertical post, crossing the line under itself.
2 Loop the line again, but this time pass the working end through the second loop and pull tight.

THE CLEAT HITCH

If you grew up on boats, chances are the cleat hitch is the first knot you learned, since it performs the rather crucial task of securing the boat to the dock. If you didn't grow up playing skipper, not to worry: this knot is easy to make. The next time you're a guest on a boat, impress the captain by tying off the boat at the end of your trip.

1 Grab the dock line leading from the boat and take a turn (knot talk for wrapping the rope around something) around the base of the cleat (the T-shaped metal anchor attached to the dock), then bring the line over the top of the cleat.
2 Wrap the line under and over the horn. This makes a figure-eight pattern over the cleat.
3 Now form an underhand loop and slip it over the horn of the cleat. Pull tight to secure.

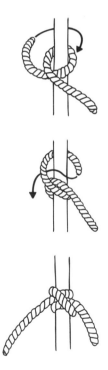

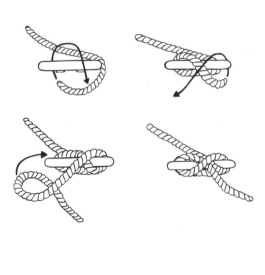

FIX A
FLAT BIKE TIRE

—

"Having been a daily cyclist for twenty years, I learned bike
maintenance through *doing* (always the best way).
Fixing a tire is one of the most important things to know as
a rider. It's seemingly easy but takes real chops. Once you
have the skill, your freedom of movement extends.
It's empowering to know that even if things go wrong on
the road, you can be back riding again in no time."

—Thomas Callahan, Horse Cycles

EASY RIDERS

Cycling is one of the first escapes you get as a child. It's that initial experience that fuels many of us to continue to ride, whether on the daily commute or to adventures further afield. In case you get a flat tire and are too far from home to limp back, here's what you need to know.

Generally speaking, there are two types of bicycle wheels: quick release and thru axle. A quick release allows you to remove the wheels without tools. Thru axles, on the other hand, require a 15-mm wrench to remove.

Once you know which bike you're working on, check the list of tools below to get you back on the road. (Note: Bike tires are rated by capacity in psi, or pounds per square inch, which ranges anywhere from 30 to 130—higher for narrow race tires and lower for thicker mountain bike tires. You can find the psi on the sidewall of the tire. Make sure to choose a pump that is at least equal to the psi of your tires.)

YOU'LL NEED
- 15-mm wrench (for thru axles only)
- Tire levers
- Spare tube
- Glueless patch kit or spare tire tube
- Hand pump (rated to your tires' recommended psi)

1 If you have a geared bicycle, place it in the highest gear (the smallest cog on the rear wheel) or, if your bike has internal gears (which change inside the rear hub), shift to the highest gear number (3, 5, 7, etc.). This allows the wheel to be removed and installed more easily, without getting tangled up in the chains, saving you time and frustration.

2 If your bicycle has rim brakes (rubber pads that hit the wheel rim when a lever is squeezed), loosen them with the lever located on the brake set, where the cable housing attaches to the brake itself. If your bike doesn't have a lever, twist the barrel adjuster (found where the cable meets the brake) clockwise to release tension on the brake cable, allowing the wheel to pass through the rubber pads.

3A If you have a wheel with an axle, use the 15-mm wrench to loosen the nuts threaded on each side, rotating the wrench counterclockwise (lefty loosey). The wheel will slide out of the frame.

3B If you have a wheel with a quick release, open the quick release. (If properly installed, it's on the nondrive side of the bike, a.k.a. the side opposite the chain.) Pulling the lever will release the wheel.

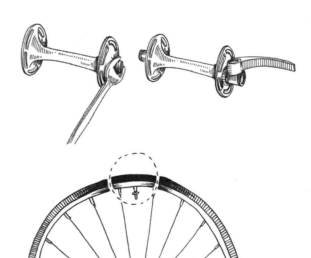

4 Gently lean your bike against a street sign, tree, or other sturdy object. Sit on the ground with the tire laid out flat in front of you. Find the valve stem (where you attach the pump to inflate your tires) and place it close to you. Pinch the part of the tire opposite the valve stem—this is the point with the least amount of tension and where it's easiest to free the bead (the inner diameter of a tire that creates a seal against the wheel rim).

5 With the tire pinched, hook the lip of the tire lever under the bead and gently pull it out and over the rim. Work your way around until one side of the tire bead is outside the rim. If the tire is very tight on the rim, use two levers.

6 Holding the valve stem, carefully reach under the now-exposed bead and pull the tube out from inside the tire. Try to maintain the orientation of the tube as it sat in the wheel, then inflate the tube with your pump to find the puncture.

7 Once you've located the puncture in the tube, check the corresponding spot on the outside of the tire for broken glass, sharp rocks, thorns, or anything else that could be the puncture culprit. Remove any debris. Inspect the inside of the tire by *carefully* dragging your finger along the inside of the tire wall, feeling for anything that could cut your new tube. Although less common, it's possible the flat occurred from a slash in the tire or everyday wear and tear. If this is the case, you're truly flat out of luck.

8 If it's indeed the tube that needs replacing, we recommend you opt for a new one, as patch kits can be tricky (although by no means impossible) to properly install. Keep a spare on hand for this reason. If you opt to use a patch kit, locate the puncture in the tube. Using the sandpaper included in your kit, scuff the surface of the cut and the immediate surrounding area to give it some tooth. Remove the backing from the glueless patch and position the center over the puncture. Firmly press and hold down the patch for ten seconds, allowing a few minutes for it to dry completely. Whether you're installing a new or repaired tube, now is the time to slide the valve through the hole in the wheel rim and place the tube gently and neatly in between the two walls of the tire. Make sure the tube isn't twisted, or else it will burst upon inflation.

→

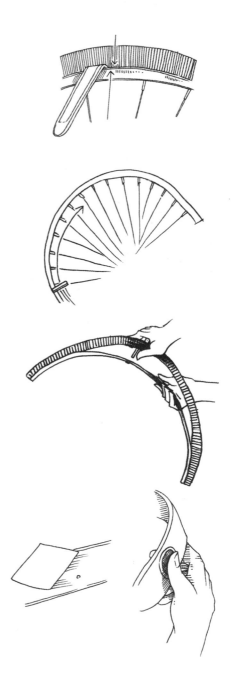

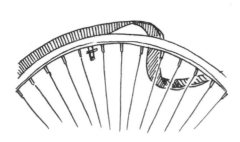

9 Starting at the valve stem, press both sides of the tire sidewall back inside the lip of the rim. From there, work your left hand counterclockwise and your right hand clockwise until they meet opposite the valve stem, where the final portion of the tire will pop back over the rim (again, it's the place of least resistance). Also check to make sure no portion of the tube got caught between the rim and the tire, as this will cause the tube to pop as well.

10 Use the pump to slowly inflate the tube. After every few pumps, remove the pump and gently spin the wheel at the axle with your thumb and index finger. While the wheel is spinning, check that the bead of the tire is correctly "seated" by making sure the line on the tire sidewall remains equidistant with the rim. (This is typically never a problem while replacing a tube, only while installing brand-new tires, but if you do have a problem, you'll need to deflate and reposition the tube inside the tire to properly seat the tire.)

11 Continue to inflate the tire to the recommended pressure.

12 To reinstall your back tire, hold the seat of the bike with one hand and the tire with the other, then slip the wheel through the rear of the frame, ensuring that the chain goes around the smallest cog of the gears. To reinstall your front tire, hold the bike by the handlebars and guide the wheel into the fork.

13 Close the quick-release lever (it should be hard enough to close that it leaves an impression on your hand) or use your wrench to tighten the nuts on both sides of the wheel.

14 With your hands, spin the wheel to make sure it rolls freely and pedal a few rotations to check that the chain is on properly.

15 Rotate the barrel adjuster counterclockwise to retighten the brake cable and position the brake pads close to the rim, and/or flip the lever. (This is essentially the reverse of step 2.)

16 Check the brakes to make sure they provide adequate stopping power. Then pedal off, happy in the knowledge that nothing in the world can slow you down.

EDC Bike Kit

Equipped with six every day carry (EDC) tools—each not much bigger than a house key—this kit is made for the self-reliant cyclist. "EDC" refers to a streamlined collection of pocket-friendly tools that go everywhere you do and tackle a variety of situations: The pair of 4-mm and 5-mm hex keys can be used to adjust the seat post or tighten the brakes. The 3-inch pry bars, made from industrial-grade steel, come in handy while changing a bike tire. And the solid brass compass glows in the dark for nighttime navigation.

READ
THE SKY

—

"There is no method of navigation more beautiful than the night sky. An ancient skill, celestial navigation is simple and efficient. In a couple of minutes, you can learn how to locate north more accurately than a compass or smartphone app. Next time you're trying to find your way, look up."

—Tristan Gooley, *The Natural Navigator*

THE SKY'S THE LIMIT

Familiarizing yourself with the stars and planets can help you keep your bearings, no matter where you are in the world. Below are some tricks for the beginner astronomer.

NAVIGATING BY THE NORTH STAR

One of the brightest stars in the sky, Polaris (or the North Star, as it's also known) never moves from its position directly over the North Pole, always shining as a beacon to true north. To find the North Star (and use it to find your way), try these easy tips:

1 The Big Dipper, a group of seven stars in the Ursa Major constellation, is a reliable reference for locating the North Star, which is the first star in the handle of the Little Dipper. Also called the Plough in Europe, the Big Dipper is essentially an arrow sign on the celestial freeway pointing toward true north. Just look for four points forming a bowl with a three-star handle attached.

2 Once you've located the Big Dipper, find the two stars that form the far side of the scoop, or dipper, where the water would pour out (should you have an infinitely enormous celestial water bucket). Then, draw a line away from the lip of the dipper straight up at a 90-degree angle. There you'll find the North Star shining brightly.

NAVIGATING BY THE SOUTHERN CROSS

If you're below the equator, you won't be able to see the North Star due to its situation directly above the North Pole. Instead, gauge your location by searching the skies for the cross-shaped constellation called the Southern Cross, or Crux. Consisting of four of the brightest stars in the southern hemisphere, it also resembles a kite. Like the Big Dipper in the northern hemisphere, Crux is a very bright, distinct formation and hard to miss on a clear night. To find true south, draw an imaginary line along the main axis, from the top to the foot of the cross. Now extend that line out another four and a half lengths. This is true south.

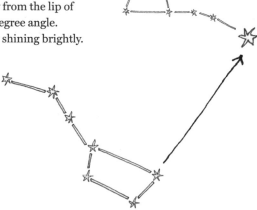

NAVIGATING BY THE SUN

During daylight hours, the sun's position in the sky is all you need to get a good sense of direction and approximate time of day. At around noon, the sun points due south in the northern hemisphere and due north in the southern hemisphere. No matter where you are in the world, it rises in the east, reaches its highest point at noon, and sets in the west.

Another simple way to navigate with the sun is to make a sundial compass. (This method requires a bit of time and patience.) Start by planting a 2- to 3-foot-long stick into flat ground, so it casts a shadow. Mark the tip of the shadow with a small pebble. Sit back and relax for fifteen to thirty minutes, or enough time for the shadow to shift. (It will always move in a rough direction from east to west.) Mark the tip of the shadow in its new position with another pebble, then draw a line between the two pebbles. The first marks west; the second, east. Stand with the first mark (west) to your left and the second mark (east) to your right. You are now facing north. This fact is true everywhere on earth.

Next time you're trying to find your way, look up.

Brass Pocket Compass

As GPS becomes more and more ubiquitous, it's easy to forget that explorers
once discovered entire continents using little more than a compass, the stars, and
their own wits. That's not to say that you need to pull out a sextant to plot your
route to work; reading a compass is simply one of those basic survival skills
to fall back on should the occasion arise. This compass, made of solid brass with
a glow-in-the-dark dial and Lexan lens, is a trusty companion for camping and
sailing trips. The cover ring is threaded to the case to create a watchlike seal,
making the compass shock- and waterproof. At 1 inch wide, it looks unassuming
but could save your life in unforeseen circumstances.

WALK
ON SNOW

—

"If you can walk, you can snowshoe, as the old adage goes.
I put easily 300 miles on my snowshoes every winter.
The sport is less daunting than skating or skiing and can be
picked up almost immediately. Just make sure your shoes
are the right size for maximum comfort."

—Amanda Weber, Iverson Snowshoes

PUT ONE FOOT IN FRONT OF THE OTHER

Invented almost six thousand years ago, the original snowshoe was made to suit the terrain it was used on. The Inuit, inhabiting the northern Arctic regions of North America and Greenland, trekked on triangular snowshoes about 18 inches long. Farther south (closer to present-day Ontario, Canada), the Cree wore a narrower snowshoe that extended almost 6 feet in length. Throughout North America, each tribe had its own design, adapted for the area in which they lived and hunted. Today's snowshoes most resemble the Huron Cree's, which included a webbed bottom and a wooden frame. This design tends to work for most hikers around the world, with variations depending on the terrain (flat, rolling, or mountainous). The shapes of modern snowshoes are made to interlock, meaning that the larger front of the shoe fits like a puzzle piece next to the back of the other shoe, making it easier to walk normally and stay balanced.

HIT YOUR STRIDE

On first try, walking in snowshoes can feel similar to walking in swimming fins. Unless the snow is a few degrees away from turning to solid ice, it will have some give, and you'll need to raise your legs higher than normal to move forward. To avoid stepping on your snowshoes or knocking them together, take longer, wider strides. With hiking poles, you can keep your balance while maintaining an easy pace. The learning curve for walking in snowshoes is very shallow, and most people can hit a comfortable stride with just a little practice.

FIND YOUR ANGLE

Walking uphill and downhill takes more skill than navigating flat terrain. Most snowshoes come with front and/or back crampons that help dig into the snow and ice, enabling a better grip on sloped ground. Hiking poles are always recommended.

For uphill walking in powdery snow, kick the tip of your snowshoe forward into the incline of the hill to create a step (otherwise known as the kick-step method), gradually loading it with your weight. Take smaller strides with your knees bent, and keep the weight of your body forward for momentum. Another option is to "side hill," a way of traversing steep and difficult terrain by pushing the uphill side of each snowshoe into the slope, creating a shelf as you move up and across. A third method is the duck walk, with shoes pointed outward at roughly 45 degrees. Pack out the snow with your foot to create a solid base before taking the next step. Regardless of which technique you use, always rely more heavily on your traction devices and poles when the snow is hard or icy. If a hill seems too steep, try finding another route before attempting what might be an impossible climb.

For downhill, take slow steps downward as you lean slightly back, planting your foot from heel to toe. Your knees should be bent. Use your poles for extra balance and better control. You may start to slide, which is okay—just be cautious of your pace. You can always stick out your butt and fall backward to halt an overly speedy descent.

If the Shoe Fits

Here's a simple equation to find your approximate snowshoe size: your weight in pounds (add in your gear, if you're carrying any) equals the same number of square inches in surface area you'll need for your snowshoe to stay afloat on the snow. For example, if you and your gear weigh a total of 200 pounds, you want about 200 square inches of surface area per shoe, which in snowshoe sizes would be 8×25 inches. For toasty toes, wear pure wool socks that wick away moisture. Go with insulated, waterproof, lace-up boots to keep your foot as secure as possible in the snowshoe bindings.

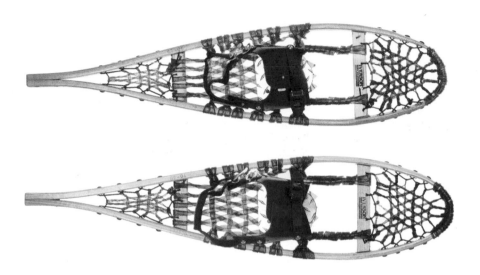

Beavertail Wooden Snowshoes

Meant for breaking a trail in soft, virgin snow, these snowshoes feature pointed tails that act like rudders, keeping your strides straight on cross-country treks. The hand-laced rawhide allows snow to sift through the knotted weave so your shoes don't become makeshift shovels that drag you down. The frames are of lightweight ash and keep their shape while remaining flexible— not to mention offering a silent step, unlike the clanking of aluminum. Each pair of Beavertails is crafted by hand in Iverson, Michigan, using a twenty-step process that includes cutting, steaming, shaping, and kiln-drying the wood on-site before the shoes are ready to float you atop a blanket of snow.

BUILD
A SHELTER

—

"As far as practical shelters go, a lean-to is the best option. When you wake up in the morning and there's hard rain beating down and harsh winds blowing, you want to feel protected. Being able to build a makeshift shelter in a pinch is an important skill that provides a psychological comfort that will help you sleep at night."

—Rob Gorski, Rabbit Island

SURVIVING IS EASY

Lean-to shelters are simple structures made of a slanted roof and two supporting columns. Their main purpose is to provide refuge to a camper without a tent, while also trapping in body heat to keep the occupant nice and warm. There are several different designs for lean-tos, depending on the size and durability you're after. We've outlined how to make an ephemeral emergency lean-to, meant to be used for a night or two and built with materials immediately available in nature.

THE BASICS

If you're stuck in the woods for a night and need to protect yourself while catching some shut-eye, an emergency lean-to should take you a few hours at most to build. Using natural materials, the basic setup includes two side posts (usually trees or large branches), a cross member, a skeleton to create the angled roof (made of strong sticks and cladding), and pine branches and debris to cover and insulate the roof. Before you start building, however, here are a few basic tips for laying the foundation:

Creature Comforts

Watch out for any creatures that might be roaming nearby. Look for tracks, droppings, and other obvious signs of animal life. If you detect evidence of larger animals, such as bears or wolves, choose a safer spot to set up camp.

Find Your Place

Choosing an already well-protected location does some of the hard work for you. Find an area that's sheltered by larger trees, a big rock, or any other natural windbreak.

Keep It Level

Finding level ground is extremely important. The rest of your structure will depend on this foundation. Even if it's an emergency lean-to, slanted ground can cause unwanted rain to trickle onto the floor.

THE BUILD

Once you've sited your lean-to, you're ready to build.

The Cross Member

After locating your side posts, choosing a cross member for the structure is extremely important. Ideally, find a long stick or fallen tree that can be placed across two lower tree branches. If the cross member can span two tree trunks but there are no branches to support it, you can use vines as cordage and tie the cross member to the two trees.

When deciding the height of the cross member, consider how much room you'll need to sit and lay down inside the shelter. There should be a few feet between you and the front of the shelter to protect yourself from any rain or snow that might enter.

The Skeleton

The skeleton is a roof structure on which a thicker layer of debris can be placed to help insulate the shelter and keep you warm. Find long, straight branches, typically pine boughs. Lean the sticks against the cross member so that the opening is opposite the prevailing winds. Make sure the angle of the branches allows you enough room to squeeze to the very back of the shelter and still fit. A 45-degree angle is usually the best option; however, you may want to create a steeper angle to shed rain or snow.

The Waterproof Weave

Weave smaller pine boughs perpendicularly through the skeleton, then weave a second course of boughs over the top, perpendicular to the first course.

The Insulation

Last, use dirt, leaves, and smaller sticks to cover your roof. The more you add on, the more waterproof the structure will be. If you build a fire just outside the shelter, the debris acts as an insulator and traps heat, making it a little warmer at night. If it snows, add a layer of snow on top of the roof, as it's a terrific insulator.

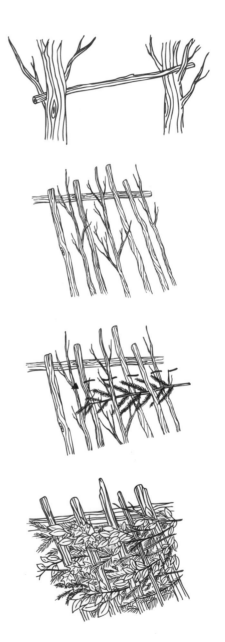

Steel-and-Leather Camping Hatchet

From the edge to the handle, this hatchet is crafted using a single,
solid piece of hardened metal, making it virtually indestructible. Strapped to
your pack, this camping tool is useful for calving off segments of small
felled trees, trimming branches on deadfall, quickly chunking wrist-size fuel logs,
and splitting and separating thin tinder and kindling. The metal darkens
with use, adding character, and the leather ages gracefully, taking
on a warm patina. In short, beyond functionality, this hardy hatchet is
a work of skilled craftsmanship.

FORAGE FOR WILD EDIBLES

—

"Every animal on earth sources food for itself, but if it weren't for grocery stores or farmers' markets, very few humans would know how. Most people don't even know the names of the plants and trees they pass on the way to work. Foraging cures what I call 'green blindness.' It teaches botanical knowledge and the awareness that nature is all around us—and a part of us too."

—Hank Shaw, author of *Hunt, Gather, Cook: Finding the Forgotten Feast*

TOP PICKS

Foraging takes equal parts acute observation and common sense. If you're a beginner, it's best to start by harvesting plants with no dangerous, inedible look-alikes. Delicious dandelions and crisp watercress are two common plants that are usually safer choices for first-time harvesters. And remember, *never* eat a plant without absolute confirmation that it is, in fact, edible.

GET SMART

If you're foraging in the United States or Canada, there is likely a Native Plant Society in your area with experts who are eager to share their knowledge. Make them your wild edible mentors; ask for advice or even a guided foraging tour of your locale. Educate yourself with websites such as naturalist "Wildman" Steve Brill's wildmanstevebrill.com, which also has a foraging app you can download for easy reference in the field; forager Sam Thayer's wonderful blog, foragersharvest.com, and book series; and educator and author John Kallas's great online resource, wildfoodadventures.com.

USE YOUR SENSES

Don't just rely on looks. Learn how to determine edible plants through smell and texture. Embrace your common sense and always forage with attention and care. If a plant smells terrible, chances are it's inedible. Does it give your skin a rash? Don't put it in your mouth. And as a general rule of thumb, almost every single plant in the world that secretes a white sap is *not* edible! So steer clear of any plant oozing white ick.

USE YOUR EYES

Plant species have a multitude of varieties, and an inedible plant could very possibly look similar to its edible cousin. Have a detailed visual reference on hand at all times to compare leaf shape, color, flowering, growth patterns, and other factors that indicate whether a plant is edible. To further help with identification, make sure the plant you plan on eating is growing at the right time of year. For example, if you spot a flowering plant in July and you're certain it should be flowering in January, it's most likely *not* the plant you think it is.

On the hunt for wild edibles, look no further than your own backyard.

AVOID THE GRIME

Don't forage for plants where there is obvious pollution in the air, water, or soil. Try to keep away from roads and parking lots, where runoff from asphalt can poison the surrounding soil. Your city park might be a great spot for a picnic, but not necessarily for picking salad greens, as most public parks use pesticides in their gardening and upkeep. Also, know the water source for your plants, especially if you want to eat your edibles raw. A polluted water source means a higher chance that the plants will contain chemicals and heavy-metal pollution. In general, the deeper in the wilderness you are, the more likely the water source is pure.

The Dandiest of Weeds

On the hunt for wild edibles, look no further than your own backyard (as long as you don't use pesticides or chemical fertilizers on your lawn). Although many of us have been taught that dandelions are weedy annoyances, the bright-faced arbiters of springtime are, in fact, a deeply cleansing plant that arrives just in time to refresh our systems after a long winter. The dandelion is a gently detoxifying bitter tonic, and all parts of the plant are widely used in herbal medicine. The bitterroot and leaf stimulate the entire digestive tract, increasing the elimination of toxins and pollutants through the liver and kidneys.

At first, the taste of dandelion greens may seem overpowering, since their bitter flavor is one of the more advanced levels of our palate. It's that very bitterness, however, that engages and stimulates our digestive systems. Younger dandelions are more tender in texture and less bitter. Throw them on a salad or down a glass of dandelion beer (once a popular rustic beverage) along with dandelion wine. You can also try roasting and grinding the dandelion root or brewing it as tea for a nutrient-rich, caffeine-free coffee replacement.

FORD
A STREAM

—

"Fording a stream is a rite of passage for anyone who wants to spend a life in the outdoors. It is one of our most primal instincts to cross water safely and get to the other side. But, like anything that takes effort, fording a body of water involves rolling up your sleeves (or pants, in this case) and getting your feet wet. In many ways a river can teach us a lot about ourselves, especially how to take the path of least resistance rather than fight the current every step of the way. If there is one piece of advice I can give, it is that crossing a river is best done naked."

—Chris Burkard, outdoor photographer

SHORE UP

If you head out into the wild, there are plenty of obvious things to worry about, from frostbite to snakebite. But what hikers might not normally take heed of are the challenges in crossing streams and rivers. Fording waterways is one of the most hazard-fraught endeavors of backcountry hiking. Plan your route wisely, arrive prepared, and follow these tips for a smooth, safe crossing.

FIND THE WATER

This may seem obvious, but before heading out onto the hiking trail, follow maps to see where the trail intersects with creeks or rivers, and be aware of seasonal flooding. If possible, call a ranger station or national-park office ahead of time to check on water levels. If you're wandering close to the ocean, carry a tide chart in your pack.

Scout Your Stream

If you're faced with an unavoidable water crossing, do your best to gauge the water depth. Carefully observe the movement and flow to check for any signs of rapids. Watch for objects jutting above the waterline to determine whether trees or other debris are blocking the way across. If you suspect there are obstacles, and if the water is deeper than your knees, try to find another place to cross.

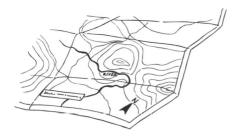

Wide Is Wise

Always try to cross a river at its straightest, widest point. Narrow spots may seem like seductive shortcuts, but many times a narrow distance between shores means deeper, faster, and more unpredictable waters. However, if you see a spot where there is an island of some sort between the two banks, that could be a safer place to cross. Islands act like dividers, splitting the current into less forceful substreams.

The Early Bird Stays the Safest

If you're crossing a glacier-fed waterway, cross as early in the day as possible. Otherwise the strong afternoon sun will have had more time to melt snow and glaciers, which can cause unpredictable water volume and dangerous currents.

Dry Boots, Happy Hiker

Always remove your hiking boots before crossing and store them somewhere high and dry. (As anyone who's had to trek in wet boots can attest, blisters form much easier in moist environments.) A gentle, sandy stream with a tolerable temperature can be traversed barefoot. If you're unsure of bottom conditions, water shoes or sandals will help protect your feet. Or double up your socks and wear them in the water. (Just make sure you've got another dry pair for the other side.)

Lean In

When you've found the best possible spot to ford, step into the water and begin moving across sideways, shuffling your feet to keep your leverage. The more contact you have with the bottom of the stream or riverbed, the more stable you'll be. Angle yourself diagonally toward the flow downstream, but facing in the upstream direction. That way, you can use the force of the water for balance rather than facing into the flow, which would make you more vulnerable to current that could potentially push you off your feet. Lean into the current slightly. Keep an eye out for bottom conditions and hidden obstacles, such as slippery, mossy rocks, the tips of jammed logs or other sharp-edged objects, and fast-flowing currents or rapids. If available, use a hiking pole or a long stick, not only for balance but to test the water depth, the flow, and the stability of the ground as you move across the body of water.

Power in Numbers

If you're hiking in a group and encounter a particularly difficult crossing, ford the water as a team. Three or more of you can form a tripod, with everyone facing in, arms locked, moving carefully across, following the method outlined above. Remember, slow and steady keeps it safe.

Rope Tricks

If you're hiking in a group and you packed a strong rope (a climbing rope is always handy), tie one end to a steady, strong tree and send the most experienced hiker/forder across first. Once across, have him or her tie the rope to a strong tree on the other side. Each subsequent hiker can hold the rope as leverage while crossing, with the last hiker (who should be the second strongest of the group) untying the rope and bringing it to the other side.

Don't Panic

We started with an obvious tip, so let's end with one. If you do fall into the water, don't panic. Instead, stay cool and collected. If the current grabs you, flip onto your back and do your best to get your feet facing downstream. If your backpack drags you down or puts you in any kind of danger, release it. Take a breath and, once the current slows, swim strongly and calmly to shore.

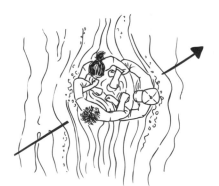

Portaging Basics

If you're traveling by canoe and hit a point in a river or stream where you need to cross by foot, lifting and carrying a canoe, known as portaging, can be a relatively simple task when done correctly. Before embarking on your outdoor adventure, practice carrying your canoe around the backyard. The more familiar you are with the canoe and how it handles, the less awkward portaging will be. Remember, technique is more important than strength.

While still on the shore, empty the canoe and place your items in your backpack or secure them, including fishing poles and anything else that's sharp and may poke or jab, to the canoe before flipping it over. There are two basic methods of portaging: the two-person lift and the one-person lift.

For a pair of portagers, one person lifts the bow of the canoe, bringing it above their head while the stern remains on the ground. The other person then gets under the canoe and places the yoke (a beam that stretches across the canoe at its center) on top of their shoulders, facing forward toward the bow. Ultimately, this person takes the canoe's entire weight and will do the actual carrying. The other person helps to spot. The process above is repeated in reverse order when the canoe needs to be placed back down.

The one-person lift is for those experienced in portage and who are canoeing on their own. Start with the canoe on the ground, tipped to one side, with the inside facing away from your legs. Stand at the center. Grip the edge of the canoe nearest to you with one hand and grab ahold of the yoke with the other, pulling it up toward you until the canoe is off the ground and resting on your bent knees. Keep holding the yoke and switch the other hand to the side farthest from your body. Then, slide the hand on the yoke to the side nearest you. Gently bounce the canoe a few times on your knees to create some momentum. When you feel ready, lift the canoe over your head in one smooth, steady movement, placing it so that the yoke sits on your shoulders with your head facing the bow.

BAIT A HOOK
AND
GUT A FISH

—

"I started fishing when I was very young. It was something
I discovered on my own, even though my father owned a boat.
I had my own secret spots on the local lake and soon
found private ponds on people's land that I would sneak onto.
At only seven or eight years old, I took my skills to the
ocean until I was old enough to buy a crappy little riverboat.
Eventually, I got my captain's license to fish offshore
in the Atlantic. Fishing is the one hobby I never let go of.
Once you learn, you might not be able to either."

—Mickey Melchiondo, Mickey's Guide Service

WHAT A CATCH

Follow these tips to get the most out of your bait.

CHOOSE YOUR HOOK

In general, the size of the hook should be more or less equal to the size of the bait you're using. You can choose between what's known as a snelled hook or a loose hook. Snelled hooks come with a pretied monofilament loop, allowing you to simply tie the filament directly to your line by knotting it through the loop. A loose hook is exactly that, loose, and can be attached by tying and knotting the hook directly to your line.

HANDS OFF

Keep in mind when baiting your hook that the less you handle the bait, the better. Human skin contains an amino acid that fish can smell and know to avoid, so keep touching to a minimum.

CHOOSE YOUR BAIT

The kind of bait you choose depends on what kind of fish you're looking to catch and in what kind of environment you're fishing. The three most common bait options are worm, commercial bait paste, and artificial bait.

Worms are used for most every type of fishing, whether mealworms, earthworms, bloodworms, sandworms—you name it. To bait the worm, thread the body from head to tail along the hook until you have more or less covered the hook with the body. Be sure to leave a small length free at the bottom for wriggling, as the worm's movement will attract the fish.

Bait paste can be purchased at most sporting-goods and fishing stores. Each paste is different and labeled according to the kind of fish it's manufactured to attract. You can also make a homemade version by mixing equal parts water, flour, cornmeal, and molasses into a thick paste and let cool. For both store-bought and homemade pastes, form into balls approximately 1 inch in circumference. Place a ball over the entire hook and press firmly into place.

Artificial bait is meant to either float on the water's surface or sink; some kinds have added metallic lures that attract fish with light, flash, and dazzle. To hook the common artificial worm–style bait, thread the hook through the top of the bait and out the bottom. Make sure the bait is firmly on the hook.

NO GUTS, NO GLORY

Here's how to clean your catch:

1 Lay a newspaper down, brown paper bag, or anything that can catch the gore and be thrown directly into a trash can.

2 Choose your weapon. In this case, the sharpest kitchen knife in your drawer, which can cut through skin, meat, and small bones.

3 Remove the scales first. If you leave them on during cooking, the flesh of the fish will go bitter. Use one hand to hold the fish by its two gills, one located behind each eye. You can also just grasp the head firmly. With your other hand, carefully scrape off the scales using a knife or fish scraper (which resembles a vegetable peeler). Always work down the fish's body from tail to head. You'll be scraping toward your hands, so be extra vigilant. Dispose of the scales in the trash.

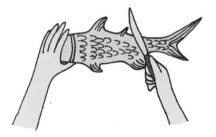

4 Remove the gills by placing your fingers under each gill and pulling firmly up and out.

5 Turn the fish on its side and use your knife to slice a smooth opening along its belly, cutting the fish almost in half from throat to tail. Using your hands, pull the fish open and remove its stomach, organs, and waste, then wash the inside of the body thoroughly with cold water. Dispose of everything in the trash.

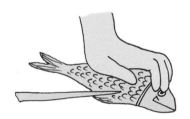

6 If you don't like the idea of cooking a fish with its head on, this is the moment you get to chopping: right where the head meets the spine, just below where the gills used to be. Remove any remaining scales or guts with cold water, then cook as desired.

Handmade American Pocketknife

For cleaning your catch out in the field, this classic pocketknife offers a sharp, straightforward combination of rust-resistant D2 steel and a canvas Micarta handle that will last for many a fishing trip for generations to come. Custom made in Oklahoma by knife maker Gene Wiseman, the compact tool is known as a sodbuster—a simple, single-bladed knife named for farmers— that's useful for any ordinary job and designed to be carried everywhere. Each knife takes two full days to produce. The slip-joint blade tucks neatly into the handle, which is smooth but not slippery, providing just enough traction while you turn that freshly caught fish into tonight's dinner.

SMOKE
FOOD

—

"Cooking is an art, baking is a science, and barbecue is a sport.
I like smoking meats because it feels like more of an
event than just making dinner. You have to gather up all your
tools, block out the day, and stock up on enough beer—
because you're going to be hanging out for eight hours
(or sometimes more). It's good if there's a game on. While you're
barbecuing, you'll want to adjust vents in case of
temperature changes, but like the pitmasters say, 'If you're
lookin', you ain't cookin'.'"

—Jed Maheu, chef

SMOKE SIGNALS

Smoking food uses a wood-fired technique that combines long cooking times with low temperatures (usually between 180 and 220°F). The result is a deeply aromatic, smoky flavor that enhances meats, fish, and veggies. Here are some tips.

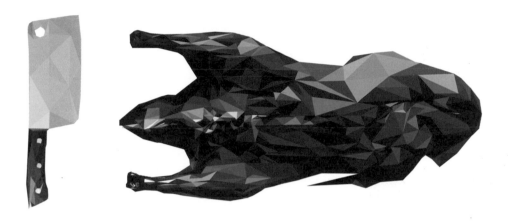

SLOW BURN

Smoking relies on patience and a low-and-slow approach. In most home-smoking scenarios, water-soaked wood chips are added to outdoor charcoal or gas grills, which are then covered and allowed to heat, smoking slowly in order to fully infuse the food with a natural smoke flavor.

DRY OR WET?

There are two distinct approaches to smoking food: dry and wet. The dry-smoking method uses a low, smoldering wood fire to slowly cook the food. Most home smoking, however, utilizes a wet-smoking or water-smoking technique, with a pan full of water placed on a rack above the heat source. This keeps the air under the grill cover moist and results in tender food.

WOOD MATTERS

The size of the wood you use when smoking affects the taste of your food. Wood chunks, for instance, smoke less and add a more delicate flavor, while wood chips burn faster and create a smokier taste. The kind of wood matters as well. If you want a subtle flavor that works with white meats, pork, and fish, try alder or a fruitwood, such as cherry or apple. If you're smoking beef, ribs, or brisket, go with bolder woods, like hickory, pecan, or oak. Mesquite is another classic smoking wood that works well with nearly all meats and vegetables.

SIX STEPS TO MAKING A SMOKIN' HOT MEAL

1   Start by soaking a handful of wood chips or wood chunks in water for an hour or more. Use this time to start your charcoal (preferably only natural rather than the "match light" variety). Heat the charcoal long enough to allow the coals to become hot and ash covered.

2   Fill a foil-lined baking pan with an inch of water and place it on a rack directly above the charcoal fire. Using tongs, add a few of your wood chips onto the charcoal. Remember, the more chips you use, the smokier your food will be.

3   Place your food onto the grill above the pan of water. Cover (and try not to peek!) for at least an hour. Keep in mind that every time you open the lid, you're sacrificing heat and smoke. Check only at hourly intervals, gauging temperature and adding charcoal briquettes. Lift the lid as needed to keep the temperature at a consistent 200°F, or thereabouts.

4   Keep a full inch of water in the pan throughout the smoking process. You can also add herbs and fruit peels, or even apple cider vinegar, to the pan of water to add greater flavor depth to your smoke. Rosemary stems work nicely with lamb and chicken. Bay leaves or orange peels also create a fragrant taste.

5   Smoking times vary greatly depending on the kind of food you're smoking, whether a cut of meat or a whole fish, as well as exactly how much food you have on the smoker. Research this in advance. For a rough idea, a whole chicken takes around four hours to smoke at 250°F, while a large salmon steak takes approximately five to seven hours at 140 to 160°F. For sliced brisket smoked at 225°F, you should calculate one and a half hours per pound of meat. We also recommend purchasing a digital meat thermometer to track temps as you smoke. To prevent your food from tasting too smoky, stop adding wood for the last half of the cooking time.

6   Once smoking is complete, remove the food from the heat and allow it to rest for around fifteen minutes before digging in and enjoying your home-smoked feast.

Note: If you're using a gas grill and it has a smoker box attached, fill the water pan and place the wood in the designated compartment before lighting the grill. If you don't have an attachment, place a foil pan directly on a rack over the heat source and follow the directions above.

KEEP THE BBQ FIRES BURNING

The minion method is a way to set up your charcoal so that it will burn for longer and at a more consistent rate. The easiest option for the home smoker is to first fill up the bottom of the grill with charcoal and a few fist-size lumps of wood. Now, fill a charcoal chimney about halfway and light the charcoal. When the coals are glowing, pour them on top of the unlit charcoal in the bottom of the grill. Adjust your vents to the desired smoking temperature (usually between 225 and 275°F). As the lit charcoal burns down, it will ignite the unlit coals, keeping the temperature steady and ensuring that you won't run out of coals before you're done cooking. Depending on the size of your grill and the amount of charcoal used, you can smoke up to eighteen hours without having to replenish the coals.

Texas BBQ Smoking Bags

Larry's Bag of Smoke is the culinary equivalent of a magician. Add one to your grill, and your food comes out deliciously smoky. The chips are sourced from a tree orchard outside San Antonio, where pecan, hickory, mesquite, and peach trees grow across 70 acres. Once a month, Larry harvests the fallen limbs, then grinds the branches to a fine consistency back at his workshop. He cuts and stitches the bags himself from bolts of cotton muslin, using the sewing skills he picked up during his navy days. Once you soak the bag in water for a few minutes and punch a couple of holes in it, it will smoke for up to four hours—imparting a taste of Texas in every bite.

THREE

Home

HOW TO

CARE FOR COPPER, SILVER, AND BRASS

—

"The first metal products of modern humankind were not tools but ornamental and decorative objects. It was the shine of metals that attracted; shine produced reflection, and reflection lets us see who we are. No surprise, then, that among the first artifacts of the Copper Age were mirrors. The meaning of humanity's metal ages can be summed up less in terms of the plows and axes with which we manifestly changed our world but rather in how we viewed ourselves."

—Mac Kohler, Brooklyn Copper Cookware

COPPER

At first glance, the patina on copper—otherwise known as verdigris, a distinctive green hue—may look like corrosion, but, in fact, this is just the metal's molecules settling into a more stable order, creating a protective layer in the process. Polishing copper, on the other hand, has the reverse effect, stirring up the molecules into a state of chaos. To keep your copper shining, here are a few helpful hints.

THE KETCHUP METHOD
Squeeze out a big glob of ketchup and mix it with salt in equal measure. Spread the solution on the copperware and work it in with a soft cotton or hemp cloth (not polyester or synthetic, as these can scratch the surface). Buff it off with another natural, soft cloth. If there's any sticky residue, rinse the copper with a little soap and warm water.

EVERY COPPER HAS A LINING
Copper corrodes when exposed to acid and is therefore always lined when made into cookware, whether with tin, stainless steel, silver, or ceramic. Test the lining of your antique copper mug or kitchen pot by applying a bit of tomato paste to the area in question. If it turns green, the lining has been breached and your cookware needs to be refitted. (You would have to ingest an exorbitant amount of copper for it to be dangerous, but better to play it safe.)

THE DARK SIDE
If you have dark spots on your copper cookware, they are likely stains from the carbon produced when water is removed from carbohydrates in starchy foods, such as pasta. Carbon and copper make fast friends and bond easily. If the stains don't come off with a good scrub, they need to be mechanically buffed, essentially breaking the carbon off the copper surface.

SILVER

The enemy of silver is sulfur molecules in the air, which, when in contact with the silver molecules, start the corroding process known as tarnishing. Tarnish first appears as a yellowish cast on the silver, eventually turning a deeper brown, then settling into a dark purple or black. The natural salts and oils on our hands also contribute to tarnishing from everyday use. Polishing the tarnish off your silver actually removes a fine layer, which is why antique silver sets are often thin and delicate, with faded engravings. Here are a few ways to keep your silver shining.

EVERYDAY CARE

To help prevent tarnish, wash your silver after each use with gentle soap and water. Dry each piece thoroughly. It's best to polish silver in the first stages of tarnish, when it's easy to remove, since a more developed tarnish will require more abrasives, depleting the integrity of your silver in the long run. A polishing cloth is very effective. Simply rub your silver with the cloth, and maintain the sheen through periodic repolishing.

GET BUFF

If you're dealing with heavily tarnished silver from an inherited (or much neglected) set, whip up your own homemade polishing paste with equal parts baking soda and water. Apply the paste to the silver with a soft cloth. Be gentle when polishing; too much force will scratch the surface.

As an alternative to buffing, use a chemical process to convert the silver sulfides (the tarnished material) back into silver. Line the bottom of a baking pan with aluminum foil and spread out your silver in it so that each piece touches the foil as much as possible. (It's fine if they touch each other.) In a separate container, add about two tablespoons of baking soda to each cup of hot water that you will need to submerge the silver. Pour the hot-water solution onto the silver in the foil-lined pan. Your pieces will start to shine up immediately, as the sulfur atoms transfer from the silver onto the aluminum. If the silver ends up looking dull, a quick buff with the polishing cloth will restore its sheen.

The ideal way to store your silver is in a dedicated cabinet that closes securely, preventing air from sneaking in. Porcelain and glass are safe companions, but keep napkins and tablecloths separate, as certain fabrics, including wool, felt, and synthetics, may carry tarnishing agents. Even natural fabrics, such as cotton, are often colored with sulfur dye. Silverware chests are typically padded with silver cloth, a special material that contains silver particles to absorb any sulfur. (Replace the cloth periodically for best results.)

If you don't have a silver cabinet or chest, wrap the pieces in acid-free paper and seal them in an airtight bag. Handle clean silver with a soft cloth (or gloves, if you're feeling fancy) to prevent transferring oils, dirt, and salts from your hands.

BRASS

Prized for its durability, brass is an alloy of copper and zinc. The ancient Greeks and Romans used brass to craft coins, jewelry, and helmets. Like copper, brass does not rust—making it a favorite of shipbuilders and seamen for centuries—but exposure to air, or natural oils and dirt in the skin, will cause the metal to oxidize and tarnish. Here are a couple of tricks to keep your brass looking its best.

FEEL THE PULL

Before you begin cleaning your brass, place a magnet on the item to see if it's solid brass or brass plated. If the magnet sticks, the object is brass plated and should only be cleaned with soap and water to prevent the brass layer from coming off. If the magnet doesn't stick, your piece is solid brass and can be more rigorously polished and cleaned, if soap and water don't do the trick.

TOP BRASS

To polish your brass, make a cleaning paste by stirring together the juice of half a lemon and a teaspoon of a natural corrosive agent, such as baking soda, salt, or flour. Apply the paste to your brass with a soft cloth and gently rub until the material's original shine comes through. Rinse all the paste off and dry immediately with a soft towel. Your brass can also be polished with ketchup (using the same method as for copper).

START AN URBAN COMPOST

—

"There aren't too many opportunities in life to create something out of nothing. Used coffee grounds, salad scraps, and that end-of-season cabbage you kept for a little too long in the fridge can actually be put to good use. A small kitchen compost creates enough nutrient-dense material to greatly enrich the soil for houseplants, backyard gardens, and tree pits, as well as cutting down on landfill. What is perhaps most exciting is the potential to contribute to and amend the landscape of a city, taking a minute to consider not just what can be grown in an urban area but also how soil health can improve the health of our immediate environment in a small way, every day."

—Cerise Mayo, Nutshell Projects

BREAK IT DOWN

Composting is a small and manageable way to live more sustainably and survive on what you essentially create for yourself. When you learn to recycle organic matter for the well-being of your plants and vegetables, you're not only reducing your waste but also enriching the soil that ultimately feeds you. A well-tended urban compost can be a clean, green decomposition machine that doesn't upset your natural habitat—or your dinner guests.

All organic matter is fair game for your compost. That means anything that was once alive or is derived from a plant or animal (eggshells, leaves, dryer lint, twigs and bark, newspaper, shredded cardboard, coffee grounds, most table scraps, etc.) Don't, however, use meat, fish, dairy, oils, bones, diseased plants, or animal manure of any sort.

The compost will be like a rich gourmet meal for your plants, and you can expect a great return for your careful, self-sufficient habits.

1   First things first: you need a solid container that will fit under the sink, or somewhere your dog can't access. Use a tall bucket (2 × 2 feet) or an old waste bin. A container with a lid is great, but a towel draped on top will also do just fine. For your scraps to compost, the mixture needs balanced exposure to air and moisture. If your pile becomes too dry, it won't break down; if it stays too wet, it turns to sludge. Ideally, your compost should be aerated from the top as well as the bottom, maintaining a level of moisture similar to a wet sponge. Air it yourself by turning the pile with a trowel once a week and adding a cup of new dirt and water as needed, or drill holes in the top and the bottom of your bucket to ensure steady air flow (or do both, which speeds up the process even more). If you make holes, drill about three each in the lid and the bottom. Don't forget to slip a small tray underneath to catch dirt and runoff. (No need to make holes in the towel, it's porous enough.)

2   The combination of "green" (nitrogen-rich) and "brown" (carbon-rich) scraps is what differentiates composting from plain ol' rot. If you only add brown scraps, it will take forever to break down; add only green, and the mixture will get very stinky as it decomposes, attracting flies and bugs. The brown-to-green ratio should always be 3:1 in terms of volume. For every three parts brown (newspaper pieces, used coffee filters, or any other paper that isn't glossy or parchment) you want one part green (food scraps).

3   If you're keeping the correct balance of nitrogen to carbon and turning the mixture regularly, your compost should be ready in a couple of months. You can then scoop it out and add it to your planters, mixing the compost with the potting soil. Make sure you're not adding big chunks of newspaper to small plant pots or window boxes, as roots will be stifled and unable to grow, causing the seeds to die. Otherwise, the compost will be like a rich gourmet meal for your plants, and you can expect a great return for your careful, self-sufficient habits.

IT'S EASY BEING ~~GREEN~~ BROWN

The method of composting recommended here is somewhere between "cold" composting (for lazy people) and "hot" composting (for people who are checking in on their compost pile every week). Your compost pile should never smell or be a hotspot for flies or bugs. If you notice any, the amount of green is slightly higher than ideal or there is some exposed green matter in there. When you add a new heap of kitchen scraps to the pile, make sure you cover it promptly with a full layer of brown materials. Keep some torn-up newspaper, used coffee grounds, or potting soil next to your compost bin to make this step easier.

MAKE NATURAL CLEANING PRODUCTS

—

"Depending on what you use to clean your home, you could be inhaling, ingesting, and absorbing toxic chemicals through your skin every day. The best way to know what's in your cleaning products is to make them yourself. Homemade cleaners are versatile, affordable, and environmentally friendly compared to the petroleum-based ingredients found in many conventional cleaning products. Try some simple recipes to reduce pollutants in you, your family, and your home."

—Lindsay Coulter, Queen of Green

CLEAN CLEANING

Safe for use on metal, plastic, chrome, steel, and ceramic, the ingredients below are likely in your cupboard already, and all are food safe. (If not, they're inexpensive and readily available.) Here's what you'll need to make your own natural cleaning products.

FIVE ESSENTIALS

- Baking soda is universally helpful due to its mild alkaline nature, which has a deodorizing effect and causes grease to become soluble in water. When not fully dissolved, baking soda also acts as a gentle abrasive for further cleaning power.
- White vinegar is a mild acid, penetrating the cell walls of bacteria and killing them off. It works as a disinfectant, grease cutter, and deodorizer. (The strong smell of vinegar dissipates after it dries.)
- Liquid castile soap is made from vegetable-sourced oils, such as olive, coconut, and jojoba, to name a few. This kind of soap works by making insoluble particles (such as grease) soluble, so that they can then be easily washed away with water.
- Essential oils, herbs, and citrus peels have some active effects, such as the antibacterial properties of tea-tree oil and the soap-scum-cutting power of lemon juice. But mainly they are a great way to naturally scent your DIY cleaning products.
- Plant-based oils (olive, coconut, jojoba) have moisturizing effects and are just as beneficial to your leather furniture and wooden cutting boards as they are to your diet and on your skin.

RUB OF THE GREEN

Where to use your natural cleaning products:

Bathroom

Pour ½ cup vinegar in the toilet and let it sit for fifteen minutes before flushing. Follow up by sprinkling in baking soda and giving the bowl a good scrub.

Fill a spray bottle with a 1:3 solution of castile soap and water. Sprinkle your tub, tiles, sink, and grout with a generous amount of baking soda, then spray the solution on top. Scrub with a brush to clean and remove stains. For marble, stone, and wood floors, mix a teaspoon of castile soap in a gallon of water (approximately 4 liters).

Clean mirrors and countertops with a 1:1 mixture of vinegar and water.

For mildew, combine 2 tablespoons of baking soda, 1 to 2 drops of essential oil, and castile soap until you have a pastelike consistency. Apply the mixture and let it sit for fifteen minutes, rinse, and wipe clean.

General Household

Sprinkle carpets, pet beds, and upholstery with baking soda fifteen minutes before vacuuming to get rid of hard-to-remove odors. Add to litter boxes and garbage cans for a similar deodorizing effect.

Make your own dust cloths by combining 1 cup water, 1 cup vinegar, 1 teaspoon olive oil, and the rind of one lemon in a jar. Let a couple of rags soak in the mixture until you're ready to put them to good use.

Note: If the smell of vinegar bothers you, add essential oils to your solutions. You can also add fresh herbs, such as mint, rosemary, lavender, and thyme, a few days beforehand to allow them to fully infuse the vinegar.

Kitchen

Soak your food containers overnight in a mixture of ¼ cup baking soda and 2 cups water to remove odors. To clean your tea and coffeepots, use a solution of 4 tablespoons baking soda and 4 cups water. Soak overnight for best results.

Scrub down your wooden cutting board with 2 tablespoons of salt and the juice of half a lemon to remove stains, then follow up with a paste of equal parts baking soda and water to remove odors. Rinse, pat dry, and rub on some olive oil to keep the wood moisturized.

The best way to know what's in your cleaning products is to make them yourself. Homemade cleaners are versatile, affordable, and environmentally friendly.

Clear the Air

Commercial air fresheners are full of carcinogenic phalates, acetone, butane, petroleum by-products, perfumes, formaldehyde, and other worrisome ingredients. Make your own custom-scented air freshener that's not only better for you but also creates a signature fragrance for your home. First, add 1 ounce alcohol (rubbing, gin, or vodka) to a spray bottle filled with about ½ cup water. Add 20 to 40 drops of your favorite essential oils. Shake to mix. Depending on the room you want to freshen up, you can create different combinations: Warm scents, such as vanilla, sandalwood, and orange, have a welcoming effect in a bedroom. In the bathroom, eucalyptus, cedar, or lavender produce a spalike environment. Bright scents, such as peppermint and lemon, help kitchens smell extra clean. Living rooms take on a cozy feel in cold months when spritzed with cedar, while rose and grapefruit give off a fresh, summery fragrance. To signal a fresh start in a new home (or an old one) or to mark a new season, burn dried sage—whether from your garden or your local health food store. This medicinal herb is believed to have a cleansing effect on a space. Place a few leaves in a ceramic bowl or any other heatproof vessel. Abalone shell is another traditional receptacle— just be careful that the burning leaves are well contained. Light the sage and extinguish the flame quickly, allowing the leaves to smolder and the smoke to clear the air.

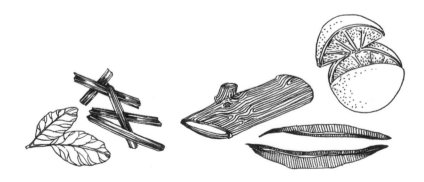

Japanese Twisty Cleaning Brush

Whether cleaning floors or scrubbing pots, this brush is up for any task.
The stiff yet flexible bristles come from the palm fibers of coconuts.
First, the coconut is harvested, cut into pieces, and soaked in water for around
a month. At that point, a machine separates the husk from the fibers,
which are by then strong and tough enough to be formed into a brush using
sturdy metal wire. The twisty shape allows for deep cleaning of harder-to-
reach spots, such as in teapots and tall drinking glasses, while the natural lipids
of palm fiber help to prevent mold and rot. Depending on how
you're using the brush, you can customize the softness by buffing the
bristles with a pumice stone.

GROW
HEALTHY
HOUSEPLANTS

—

"Houseplants are more than just decoration; they serve
a powerful function, too. Their mere presence makes us happier
and healthier. They also actively clean and *make* the air
we breathe, eating our indoor air pollutants [volatile organic
compounds, or VOCs] and turning the carbon dioxide
we exhale back into oxygen. It's a beautiful cycle. Just two
healthy houseplants can clean the air in a 10 × 16 foot room.
Add some greenery to your home and breathe easy."

—Stephanie Bartron, SB Garden Design

RULES OF GREEN THUMB

Houseplants generally prefer moderate to hot indoor temperatures (50 to 80°F), so if you live somewhere very cold, keep them away from drafty doors and windows and out of unheated rooms. This applies in offices and classrooms too: plants will suffer when the heat is turned off at night or on the weekends. Regular watering is also important, but overwatering is often as bad as underwatering. For most houseplants, let the soil dry out on the surface. You can stick your finger into the dirt to check moisture. If it's dry below the top inch of soil, or if the plant is wilting and looking less green, it's time to water.

WHEN TO WATER

To keep plants well hydrated, set up a watering schedule by picking one day a week and watering all of your plants deeply. (Some say not to water at night, as that can encourage bad microbes in the soil, but if you water infrequently and let the soil dry between waterings, this shouldn't be a problem.) When adding water, the whole surface of the soil should be wet—but not overflowing—and the water should soak into all the roots. (You can gently lift up the pot to check for moist, happy roots through the drain hole.) Watch the saucer, or outer container, for any overflow, which can be emptied into the next thirsty plant that needs watering.

Many houseplants are tropical, so ice-cold water can hurt them—and boiling water will kill most plants. (It's therefore an effective organic weed control.) A few ice cubes left on the soil works great for watering smaller plants, since the cubes melt slowly, reducing shock to the plant's system. This method is often recommended for orchids, which need just a little water at a time. For most other plants, let the water sit and adjust to near room temperature before pouring. Filtered or harvested rainwater is helpful in limiting or avoiding salt and mineral buildup in the potting soil. Some plants are more sensitive than others, and some municipal water supplies contain more minerals than others. Using filtered water avoids the issue, plus it's a great way to recycle extra water (that half-full pitcher of drinking water you were about to empty in the sink, for example). If your houseplants live outside during the warmer months and you get summer rains, let them soak in the clean rainwater. This will leach out any salts and minerals that may have accumulated from hard tap water.

If you keep a worm farm or compost, give a few tablespoons to your plants once a year. If your plants are looking less green than usual and aren't thirsty, give them a mild organic indoor plant fertilizer (available at your favorite nursery) and follow the instructions for dosage and application.

CREATE YOUR GREEN OASIS

Tips for arranging different types of plants throughout your home.

SUN WORSHIPPERS

If you have a sunny spot close to a window where the plant will receive at least four hours of direct sunlight a day, try these options:

Lucky Bamboo

This plant is not really bamboo (which is too big and needs too much sun to be kept in small indoor spaces), although it does look similar. Usually it comes planted in pebbles, but you can replant the lucky bamboo in soil, in which it will ultimately be happier and probably live longer. Water every few days, and if it starts to smell "swampy," empty and clean the container and let the plant dry out for a few days before refilling with clean water. (Occasional dryness keeps bad bacteria in check.)

Aloe Vera

Every home should have aloe on hand for kitchen burns and sunburns. The dwarf variety is best for a houseplant, as it needs less sun and grows to a more manageable size than its larger cousins. Keep it outside during warm summer months and bring it inside well before the first frost. (It's hardy down to around 50°F.) Like most succulents, the aloe needs to dry out completely between waterings and only requires water once a week at most. It will spout new "pups" from its root system, which you can separate and repot to share with friends.

Kalanchoe

These tropical plants are widely available, mostly year round, and flower in many bright colors. Keep them moist to prolong the blooms, and cut off any dead (brown) flower clumps. Once all the flowers are gone, let the plant rest (water infrequently), or compost it and start over. If you want the plant to rebloom annually, put it outside during the summer months, water regularly (at least weekly), and feed it some compost or other balanced organic plant food every two weeks from March to August.

MADE IN THE SHADE

If you have a spot that's away from direct light but not in total darkness (ideally with four to eight hours of indirect, bright light with the curtains open or from full-spectrum lightbulbs every day), try one of these options:

Pothos

This is a good plant for wall planters, hanging baskets, and the top shelf, as the leaves hang down from vines rather than stiff branches. When the vining branches grow too long, especially if they start sprouting aerial roots, trim them to your desired length. To make more plants, remove the leaves along the bottom few inches of the cuttings and stick the vines in water for a few weeks. Once the roots appear, you can plant the rooted cuttings in soil. Water regularly and share your new plants with friends.

Snake Plant

These plants are more tolerant of darkness than most, so if you're worried that your room might not get enough light, this is a good plant to try out. It's forgiving as long as you water it deeply at least once a month. Whether you buy the variegated (with a yellow-green edge) or the solid-green variety, it's easy to care for.

Spider Plant

The bright, green-and-white-striped strappy leaves of this plant look great growing out of a tabletop pot, on a plant stand, or as a hanging plant. Long stems shoot out from the base and drape down, sprouting small flowers, which quickly become little "plantlets." You can leave these to grow on the plant, or cut the stems at their base, break off the plantlets (which will have tiny aerial roots sprouting), and plant them in their own pots. You'll never be without a gift.

CACTI AND AIR PLANTS

Cacti need to rest in the winter, as they would in the wild. This means that you should water them less often and move them away from bright light but not where they might freeze (aim for a room that stays 40°F or warmer). If you like to give them fertilizer to ensure flowering, don't do it in the winter. (It's like serving them coffee at night—not very restful.) In the summer, you can move the cacti outside once nighttime temps stay above 50°F.

Air plants generally prefer regular, bright light year round. Every other day, spritz them thoroughly, or submerge them completely in a weekly bath of room-temperature rain- or filtered water. Mix some air-plant food into the shower or bath if you want to encourage them to bloom again.

STOCK
A TOOLBOX

—

"Growing up, my father was a framing foreman and novice box maker, so I began working with wood at a very young age. We would build fun little projects in the garage when I was a little kid, and by the time I was fourteen, I was working on commercial job sites doing simple tasks and learning the basic tools of the trade. I was drawn to custom furniture making because it requires good engineering and good design. You have to use both sides of your brain."

—Shaun Wallace, Gopherwood Design/Build

GIVE YOURSELF A HAND

When it comes to stocking your toolbox, the box itself will be a key fixture in your workshop. Be sure to select one that features organizers and dividers, so that each tool has its own special spot, making things easy to find and store. Once you select your container, take a look at the following list. These are the top ten basics that belong in every toolbox—but don't feel pressured to buy everything at once. Instead, choose your tools with care and invest in higher-quality items each time a new project calls for it. You'll save in the long run.

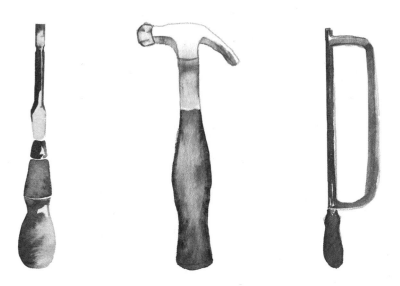

1 Claw hammer. You'll use the stalwart claw hammer for everything from basic home repair to picture hanging to specialized carpentry and beyond. To start, go for the classic 16-ounce hammer. A wood handle feels good in the palm and, unless you're on a serious demolition mission, holds up to any task. Always check the balance of a hammer before you buy it, making sure it's neither too heavy nor too light.

2 Screwdrivers. The flathead screwdriver has a single blade for screwing and unscrewing flathead screws—a must for any toolbox. It can also be used to pry open stuck paint can lids and for other quick fixes when you're in a jam. In addition to the flathead, you'll want a Phillips head screwdriver for Philips head screws. Screwdrivers come in a variety of sizes and shaft lengths. See what feels best in your hand; each tool should have heft and balance. To save a bit of space in your box, try an all-in-one screwdriver, which has multiple tips that easily switch out and are usually stored in the handle of the screwdriver itself.

3 Adjustable wrench. There are different wrenches for different jobs, but an adjustable model is a tool you'll reach for often. (It's particularly useful for plumbing jobs.) Featuring an offset head, the adjustable wrench loosens and tightens nuts and bolts of different sizes, making it a handy multitasker.

4 Tape measure. A good rule of thumb for choosing a tape measure is to go for the heavy-duty, 16- to 25-foot metal variety. They usually come in varied widths (from ½ inch to 1 inch); wider ones are generally easier to use with one hand. A tape measure will help with most at-home needs, such as measuring blinds or drapes, or making sure that new sofa will actually fit up the stairs, through the door, and into the living room.

5 Level. A level is a simple tool to ensure precise horizontal alignment down to the millimeter, for everything from framed photos to shelving to flatscreen TVs. (Your eye can be tricked by a crooked floor or sloped ceiling.) A 3- to 4-foot metal level can also double as a straightedge.

6 Saw. A basic hacksaw is all you need for small woodworking tasks. Hacksaws are sturdy and sharp enough for cutting through thinner wood, plastic, and metal. Most of your everyday home repair issues can be tackled with a standard high-tension model, which usually features a sturdier frame and a high-tension blade for easier cutting.

7 Pliers. Needle-nose pliers, in particular, are great for extracting, pulling, or tugging anything stuck in a tight spot. You might also want to stock adjustable pliers, which lock into place and can be used as clamps and wire cutters.

8 Utility knife. An all-in-one, all-around handy tool, the trusty utility knife does everything from sharpen pencils to slice open boxes and cut through upholstery fabric. Look for one with built-in blade storage.

9 Cordless drill. You'll be surprised how often you pick up your drill. A good cordless model will go anywhere and help you drill holes, drive screws, and more. Depending on the kind of bit you use, drills can make light work of grinding, sanding, and stirring.

10 More toolbox essentials. A few extras to keep in your home repair arsenal: sandpaper, tape (masking, duct, electrical), nails in assorted sizes, screws in various widths and lengths, glue (wood, all-purpose, and super), work gloves, paint rags, and safety goggles. A picture hanging kit, which usually includes hangers and wire suited for hanging light- to medium-weight artworks, is also great for last-minute decorating.

Solid-Steel-and-Leather Hammer

Capable of driving and extracting nails with remarkable ease,
the 16-ounce Estwing leather claw hammer is the superhero of the toolbox
and a product of true craftsmanship. While many other hammers are
manufactured as two separate pieces (head and handle), the Estwing is forged
from a single piece of steel. Add to that a bound and lacquered leather
handle, and you have a shock-absorbing, long-lasting, well-balanced workhorse
of a tool that's made to tackle a wide variety of everyday household fixes.

MAKE
A FLORAL
ARRANGEMENT

—

"Flowers create shapes that happen on their own; at
a certain point, you have to just stand back, let go, and trust.
Things won't always turn out exactly the way you
want them to. But that's what's beautiful about the whole thing.
The impermanence of your creation forces you to relax.
And it's such a treat to have a new palette, a new bloom, to play
with every time you start a new arrangement."

—Lisa Przystup, James's Daughter Flowers

IN FULL BLOOM

Learning how to work with flowers allows you to play with texture and color. It also makes you notice aesthetic details you might never have otherwise: the line of a stem, the curve of a petal, a nuance of form. Here are our tips for arranging and caring for your blooms.

YOU'LL NEED

- A medium-size vase that fits approximately ten to fifteen flowers
- A 5 × 5 inch square of chicken wire, or enough to create a ball that fits snugly in your vessel of choice
- Clippers

1   Form a ball of chicken wire with your hands that fits into the bottom of the vase. This will keep the flowers in place. Make the ball loose enough for the stems to slip easily through the holes. Next, fill the vase with water. If it's made of clear glass, you may want to secure the chicken wire over the opening with tape to create a grid pattern that's hidden from view.

2   Add greenery to establish an asymmetrical base, followed by your "statement" flowers (roughly three to five). Then add your secondary flowers, which help support and accent those larger primary blooms—and can sometimes steal the show altogether. If you're not happy with the front, spin the vase around. Sometimes looking at the arrangement from another angle reveals something you didn't see before.

→

3 Construct layers and build up. For example, cut one flower long and another just a bit shorter. The shorter flower will rest below the longer one while simultaneously hiding its stem. There are no hard-and-fast rules to arranging flowers. Some of the most beautiful arrangements have a lot of negative space and unruly stems sticking out here and there. The general idea is to keep the eye moving. There should be a natural movement to the arrangement that keeps it visually interesting.

4 How do you know when it's done? When you start to fuss, walk away.

KEEP IT FRESH

You're working with a perishable item, so there's no magic trick for drastically extending its freshness. That said, there are several things you can do to make sure your blooms don't wilt too quickly.

- Trim the stems with a sharp tool just before you add them to the vase. Dull blades can crush the stems, and the bloom won't hydrate as efficiently. Also, trim the stem at an angle, so the opening/surface from which the flower hydrates is larger. Don't forget to trim the greenery too.
- Keep the flowers in a cool place, out of direct sunlight.
- Some people advocate using bleach or Sprite to prolong an arrangement's vitality, but we say changing the water daily is a simpler (and a more natural) method.

A Note on Budgeting

Playing around with inexpensive flowers before splurging on more exotic blooms is a sensible way to build your flower-arranging skills. Balance the cost of a few especially beautiful or hard-to-find blooms from the florist with simple bouquets from the local corner shop. Carnations, roses, and chrysanthemums are all great basics, complement most flowers, and are readily available.

Royal Sussex Garden Trug

Handmade in England since 1829, this shallow basket is a "modern"
take on the Anglo-Saxon trog, a heavy, boat-shaped wooden vessel used by
farmers until the mid-seventeenth century. Queen Victoria discovered
the trugs at the Great Exhibition in London in 1851 and personally placed
an order, giving it a royal stamp of approval. Today, the materials and fabrication
processes remain unchanged. Strong, rot-resistant sweet chestnut wood
is shaved and bent to form the handle and rims, which are fastened together
with copper nails to create the frame. Light enough to cradle in your
arm while you gather greenery in the garden, these trugs also make a quick
tabletop centerpiece when filled with flowers.

FRAME
AND
HANG ART

—

"Framing a drawing, print, card, photo, or anything else that's special to you is a way of honoring its existence, elevating it from a piece of paper to a piece of art. A frame acts as an archival capsule, keeping your memento safe from dings, ripped edges, and the slow damage of time. Choosing a frame is subjective. I tend toward simple, black wood, allowing the piece to take center stage. Although I do have a few tiny etchings and doodles framed in some gold, behemoth frames. Trust your eye and use your imagination."

—**Amy Jo Diaz, production designer**

THE LOST ART OF FOUND FRAMES

If you've decided to forego a store-bought frame, we recommend scouring thrift and antique stores for vintage frames that possess a bit more character than manufactured faux-wood options. You'd be surprised how many beautifully ornate frames are languishing at your local Salvation Army. Once you've found the frame that suits the art you're set to hang, follow these basic framing steps.

YOU'LL NEED

- Artwork of choice
- Found, premade frame with glass included
- Mat paper cut to the same size as the frame glass (acid-free mat paper is best and can be found at most art and craft supply stores)
- Mat cutter, if you choose to cut the mat paper yourself (most framers will custom cut mat paper to order for relatively cheaply)
- Artist's tape (acid-free artist's tape is best and can be found at most art-and-craft-supply stores)
- Several small ½-inch nails
- Hammer
- Ruler
- Screwdriver

OPTIONAL

- Craft paper and glue for covering the back of the frame
- Picture wire and D-rings, if your found frame is missing these essential elements
- A paint or stain of your choice, if you're opting to repaint or restain your found frame

1 Prep your frame by cleaning the glass and wood thoroughly. Allow them to dry completely before starting the framing process.

2 Mat your art. Some like to place the art directly on top of a larger mat, with enough room around the edges to act as a frame. Others prefer to have a window cut out of the mat, with the art placed directly behind it. If you want to cut the mat paper yourself, use a paper cutter and ruler to cut an appropriately sized window for your art. Try to form a frame that covers just the very edge of the artwork so that you're enhancing, rather than hiding, it. (As mentioned previously, you can also take the mat paper to a framer to have it custom cut.)

→

3 Center your art behind or on top of the mat paper. Most professional framers center the image horizontally but leave a bit more room at the bottom of the artwork than at the top, which is gallery standard (but by no means obligatory).

4 Once the art is centered, you can use the "hinge" mounting technique, which allows you to suspend the artwork without damaging it. (Note: this only works for artwork mounted behind the mat paper.) Start by flipping both mat and artwork to face downward, ensuring that the art is still centered. Take a 4-inch strip of artist's tape and place it equally over the top-left edge of the artwork (roughly 2 inches in from the outer edge) and onto the mat. Repeat on the right side, again placing the tape equally over the artwork and the mat, about 2 inches in from the outer edge. Now your two tabs of tape should connect artwork and mat, creating a hinge. To reinforce, apply small horizontal strips of tape over both vertical tabs. This method helps to conserve the artwork by minimizing its contact with adhesives and allowing the mat paper to breathe rather than buckle and ripple. (For this reason, you should never tape the entire length of the artwork to the mat.)

5 Now it's time to place the glass into the frame, doing your best not to cover it with fingerprints. Lay in the mounted art. Finish by putting the back of the frame into place and gently hammering it with ½-inch nails every 6 inches or so around the frame to keep it secure.

Optional: You can also cover the back of your frame with craft paper, found at most art supply stores. Cut the paper to size and use wood glue to attach it to the backside of the frame. If your frame needs new picture wire, simply use your screwdriver to place two D-rings on each vertical side of the frame at about the halfway point. Thread and twist the wire through each ring, making sure the wire is taut and strong.

Wall Power

How do you arrange your frames when adding to your wall art collection? Don't be afraid to mix and match size and shape, hanging the frames in clusters of three or five (odd numbers create a nice shape). This can lend a rich and textured look to your home gallery. No need to measure the spaces in between—eyeballing it works just fine, and you can adjust as needed once you see the whole. When selecting art to showcase, resist your instinct and try *not* to make the grouping overly uniform, as it can look too controlled and art directed. Instead, pair photos with illustrations, paintings with woodcuts, embroidery with mirrors. If you chose and love the art, chances are the wall will feel unified by your own particular aesthetic.

THE SCIENCE OF HANGING YOUR ART

If framing is an art, then hanging is a science. Before you start, consider the size of your framed art, its placement, its weight, and the optimal height. After all, you want to give your work a steady and sturdy home for all to see.

YOU'LL NEED

- Framed art
- Hammer
- Level or ruler
- Hooks gauged to your artwork

Rule of thumb: A one-nail picture hook holds about 30 pounds or less. A two-nail picture hook will hold up to about 50 pounds. If you've got a massive art piece heavier than 50 pounds, a three-nail picture hook is the way to go. Use two picture hooks per artwork to keep the piece stable and level.

OPTIONAL

- Construction paper
- Artist's tape
- Thumbtacks

1. A helpful way to find that perfect placement before committing to hammer and hooks is to cut a piece of construction paper to the approximate size of your framed art. Using artist's tape or a thumbtack, adhere the paper to the wall at the exact spot you're thinking of hanging your art piece. Step back. Does it look and feel right? Move the paper around, playing with height and its balance with the other objects and art in the space.

2. When hanging heavier pieces, tap the wall gently to find the sturdy studs behind the drywall, which will offer your artwork more support. A hollow sound means no stud, a dull thump means there is one. (Or eliminate the guesswork by using a stud finder.)

3. Measure and lightly mark a spot on your wall, close to the studs and with the center of the picture approximately 57 inches from the floor—eye level for most people. Don't feel tied to this rule, however. Place the art where it feels right to you.

4. Hammer the two picture hooks into the wall, equidistant from the vertical center of the frame and on the same horizontal level. Be sure to hammer into studs if your art is on the heftier side. You can use a level or ruler to align the hooks.

5. Hang your art by its picture wire onto the picture hooks. Step back and admire the beginnings of your self-made gallery.

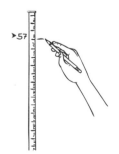

MAKE
CANDLES

—

"I enjoy creating art that celebrates process.
Making candles allows you to be experimental, because
wax is very expressive. For me, candle making is an
art form that communicates positivity. To be able to give
the gift of light is very rewarding."

—Wendy Polish, le Feu de l'Eau

GUIDING LIGHTS

For five thousand years, we've been making tiny torches for a multitude of uses—first for light and then for atmosphere. All candles function in a similar manner: fire burns wax and wax soaks into the wick, becoming the oil that fuels the flame. Candle wax usually consists of either plant-based oil or animal fat, but for our purposes we're using traditional beeswax, which burns cleanly and has a naturally warm, honeyed scent.

Following this recipe, a pound of beeswax will make approximately four 4-ounce candles, and you should have extra wax for at least a few more.

YOU'LL NEED

- 1-pound block of beeswax
- Sharp carving knife or cleaver
- Cotton string or premade wicks
- Double-sided adhesive tape
- Disposable chopsticks (or something to use as stir sticks)
- Two tall drinking glasses
- Double boiler
- Glass or metal containers of your choice (vintage Mason jars, recycled jam jars, or whatever can tolerate the heat of melted beeswax)
  Note: *If you want to avoid getting your favorite cookware covered in wax, simply place a used coffee can in a large, shallow pot of water. Or invest in a traditional wax-pouring pot that's made specifically for melting candle wax.*

OPTIONAL

- Essential oils, such as lavender, rosemary, or cedar, for additional scent

Candle making is an art form that communicates positivity. To be able to give the gift of light is very rewarding.

1. Chop up the block of beeswax into small, 1-inch cubes.

2. Melt the beeswax pieces in your double-boiler rig on low heat (around 125°F is optimal). Stir occasionally with a metal or wooden spoon, keeping in mind that the wax will be hard to remove, so use a spoon that you don't mind sacrificing to the cause or a disposable wooden chopstick or skewer. Add in essential oils if you're scenting the candles.

3. Prep your wick and container. If you're using premade wicks, simply use the double-sided adhesive tape to adhere the wick to the bottom center of your candle vessel, leaving a few inches of string extending beyond the top. If you're using cotton string, dip it quickly into the melted wax to create a solid coating. Allow it to cool, then adhere the string to the bottom center of the container with double-sided tape, again leaving a few inches at the top. Gently holding the wick upright, wrap the extra length around your spoon or disposable stirrer.

4. Here is where you use your two drinking glasses as a method to hold the wick upright in the container. Prop the stirrer horizontally across the top of the two glasses, taping it down for extra stability. The goal is to hold the wick up through the center of the candle container. You may want to put your prepped container on top of a cutting board or trivet to protect your counter from the heat.

5. Once the wax has thoroughly melted, carefully pour it (remember, this is hot stuff!) into your container, making sure to not let the wax splash. Go slowly and methodically. Fill the container almost to the top, keeping in mind that the wax will contract a bit as it cools.

6. Allow your candles to sit and cool overnight, then unwrap the wick from its stirrer/two-glass setup (and remove the tape, if you used it). Then snip off the extra length so your wicks are about ½-inch tall. Now it's time to impress your friends with your candle-making prowess. Give the candles as gifts, or use them as centerpieces at your next dinner party.

Polished-Brass Candle Holder

If you make tealight-size candles (the molds are readily available),
place one in this brass holder and watch the polished surface subtly reflect
the light of the flame. Made in Sweden by a four-hundred-year-old
brass foundry, the small vessel adds extra warmth to a space and amplifies
the glow of your homemade creation.

CARE FOR WOOD

—

"My earliest days working with wood were as a kid, whittling kindling with a pocketknife by a campfire in the mountains of North Carolina. I'd peel the bark away and carve along the existing shape of the sticks. I never forced them to become something different than what they were. I still take that approach today with my furniture: every board I use brings its own identity and history. The wood probably manipulates me more than I do it."

—Casey Dzierlenga, Dzierlenga F+U

GO WITH THE GRAIN

Whether a bright pine floor in the afternoon sun or a walnut rocking chair glowing by the fire, wood adds a beautiful, natural warmth to a room. Caring for your wood starts by identifying the variety: teak, for instance, needs to be oiled on occasion, while walnut only requires a soft-cloth cleanse. (If you're unsure of the kind of wood you have, the website wood-database.com is a reliable resource for identification.) Once you know the wood and its particular wants and needs, just keep a few of these simple tips in mind, and always start with a gentle cleansing, using a very soft, lint-free cotton cloth.

DUST NEVER DIES

Try to dust all your wood furniture weekly; even a small buildup of dust and dirt can scratch wood's delicate finish. A lint-free cloth or lamb's wool duster is best for your wood, since the lanolin in sheep's wool will most efficiently collect the dust particles. If you're using a feather duster, be gentle, as the feather shafts can sometimes scratch delicate wood finishes. You can also try what's called a tack cloth, available in the painting section of most hardware stores. Tack cloth pulls dust away from the wood and onto its own sticky surface.

WIPE THE SLATE CLEAN

A simple soap-and-water combo is the best way to clean dirt from wood. Add a capful of gentle detergent to a sink or a pail of lukewarm water, dampen and wring out a soft cloth, then wipe quickly over surfaces, being careful not to let the water soak into your wood. Wipe off any excess moisture with a fresh, dry cloth.

(UN)MAKE YOUR MARK

Trying to remove water rings or hazy spots on your coffee- or dining-room table? A very mild abrasive, such as a teaspoon of baking soda dissolved in a cup of water, should do the trick. Another method is to rub the area with a small amount of mayonnaise using a dry, soft cloth. (Whereas pure vegetable oil would stain your wood because it dries too quickly, the consistency of mayonnaise keeps the area moist and gives the vegetable oil time to penetrate.)

If your table is finished with a light wax, try the heat technique: Place a dry, soft cloth on top of the water ring and heat your clothes iron to medium. Iron the cloth gently, always moving, for about ten seconds at a time, lifting often to check progress. The gentle heat will dissipate the water rings trapped in the top layers of the wax.

THAT'S THE SPIRIT

If you need a more thorough cleaning of particularly grimy wood, try mineral spirits, which can be found at most hardware stores. A form of turpentine, mineral spirits help remove stubborn grease and dirt. Press your cloth against the top of the spirits container and soak as you would a cotton ball. Use firm, circular strokes. If you prefer to use a natural wood cleaner, mix together a tablespoon of olive oil, a tablespoon of water, and the juice of one lemon. Place a small amount of the mixture on a soft cloth and get to cleaning the green way.

SHINE ON

If you want extra shine, you can follow up a basic cleaning with polishing. Choose a gentle polish specifically formulated for wood and use it according to the instructions. Keep away from run-of-the-mill spray and cream polishers that contain silicon, since they can ultimately damage wood as the silicon soaks directly into the grain.

ADD A COAT

Every six months or so, supplement cleaning with a protective treatment. Our favorite is conventional butcher's wax, made with beeswax, to keep your wood durable and stain resistant. Or, if the wood has a more fragile finish, try an acid-free microcrystalline wax. (The downside: it costs a bit more and is less friendly on the environment.) Start by cleaning surfaces thoroughly and allowing the wood to dry. Next, use two soft, lint-free cloths: one to apply a thin coat of wax to the wood, the other to polish. Put some elbow grease into it!

TOO HOT TO HANDLE

Whenever possible, arrange your wood furniture away from direct sunlight and heaters. Heat will destroy wood finishes, as well as dry and shrink the wood, ultimately causing it to crack. If you reside in a particularly dry climate, we recommend using a humidifier in the winter.

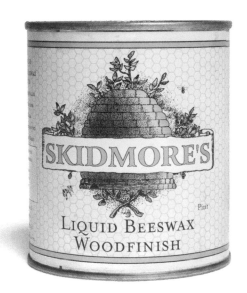

Beeswax Wood Care and Finish

Manufactured in Wyoming, Skidmore's was created by the woodworker
and craftsman Vincent Skidmore in 1987. The handcrafted beeswax polish seals
and protects untreated and new wood while adding a soft, glowing finish.
It enhances the grain of both indoor and outdoor furniture, as well as wooden
floors and decks (or even a redwood hot tub or sauna). The polish
helps remove white rings and water stains, gently cleansing, restoring,
and recapturing the former glory of your favorite wood pieces.

MAKE
HERBAL HOME
REMEDIES

—

"For humans, healing happens on many levels, and the same is true of plants. Healing comes from the specific characteristics in the chemical makeup of a plant and from the specific nutrients and minerals it pulls out of the soil. Plants, especially herbs, have many medicinal qualities, offering us a multitude of healing techniques through everything from their varied chemical blends and leaf textures to flower color and the potency of their seeds and roots."

—Melinda Joy Miller, Shambhalla Institute

GOOD FOR WHAT AILS YOU

Here are a few simple home remedies. They are traditional medicinal cure-alls, passed down through generations, using plant-based ingredients from your garden, kitchen, or fridge to sooth all sorts of everyday ills. Always be certain before taking a plant-based remedy that you are not allergic to the ingredients.

SCRAPES, CUTS, AND BURNS

There are a multitude of natural soothers for scrapes and burns, but lavender essential oil is one of the most practical and potent. Not only is it antibacterial and antiseptic, it's also calming to the skin. To apply, soak a cotton ball with the oil (available at most health food stores) and apply directly to scraped skin. Lavender will simultaneously disinfect the wound and temper the pain.

A live aloe vera plant is always good to have on hand for treating unexpected scrapes, cuts, and burns. Cut an aloe leaf off at the base of the plant. (The outer leaves are the oldest and therefore contain the most amino acid–rich gel.) Slice the leaf in half and gently scrape out the gel. Rub it onto any sort of skin irritation, from mosquito bites to sunburns, for an instant cooling and soothing effect.

Another easy home fix for sunburned skin comes in the form of the everyday potato. Idaho, Red Bliss, no matter—each type possesses starch, which helps to soothe skin that's been in the sun too long. Simply wash and grate two or three raw potatoes into a cup, adding a splash of water. Rub the mixture directly onto sunburned skin and allow it to dry before washing off.

UPSET STOMACH

The key ingredient in most commercially made, over-the-counter stomach soothers is likely sitting somewhere in your pantry or at the back of your refrigerator. Bicarbonate of soda, or baking soda, reacts with stomach acids to help quell upset tummies and indigestion. Dissolve a teaspoon of the baking soda in a cup of warm water and drink for near-immediate relief.

Fresh, sliced ginger or a handful of fresh peppermint soothes the stomach when steeped in hot water as a tea. Your spice rack is a natural source for relief as well. Chew on a few raw fennel seeds to aid digestion after a heavy meal.

POISON IVY AND OTHER RASHES

Your pantry holds natural remedies for calming skin irritations and rashes. If you come into contact with poison oak or ivy, mix equal parts baking soda and white vinegar and apply the paste directly to the affected area. Leave the mixture on the rash until it dries completely. Rinse with lukewarm water, as hot water can further inflame the skin.

To relieve itchy skin or rashes, try drawing a lukewarm bath, adding in ½ cup of raw oats (wrap in cheesecloth to prevent making a mess of the tub), a tablespoon of baking soda, and 2 cups of white wine vinegar. Dip in and relax while the trio of ingredients works to moisturize, soothe, and calm your skin.

SORE THROATS AND COUGHS

When it comes to the occasional cough and sore throat, there is no more powerful pairing than honey and garlic. Honey, with its antibacterial qualities, is a highly versatile natural medicine. Garlic, an antiviral and antifungal, is another potent ally against colds, coughs, and flus. Start by peeling and chopping 3 to 4 cloves of fresh garlic. Mix the cloves in a cup of honey and leave overnight, or for around twelve hours. Take one teaspoon of the honey-garlic concoction twice a day, every day, until the cough has dissipated.

Another tried-and-true method for kicking coughs and sore throats is to gargle with salt water. Stir a teaspoon of salt (natural sea salt is best) into a glass of warm water until it dissolves. Gargle with the mixture—but don't swallow, as salt can upset the stomach. Repeat every few hours.

EARACHES

A few drops of warm olive oil is a simple remedy to combat earaches naturally. Begin by heating about ½ cup of olive oil over very low heat, just until it is warm to the touch. Be careful not to overheat. Once the oil is warmed, use a clean dropper to place a few drops directly into the ear. The warm oil soothes inflammation within the eardrum and helps flush out trapped mucus, the cause of most common earaches.

HEADACHES

The first and most obvious home remedy for a headache is a glass of water. Dehydration is often the culprit, so drink a glass or two as soon as you feel that first throb of pain in your temples.

If this doesn't do the trick, another simple way to alleviate a headache is by preparing an at-home steam. Grab a large pot, fill with water, and bring to a boil. Add in a handful of fresh herbs, such as lavender, rosemary, peppermint, and basil. Try a combo of all, or a few—each works as a decongestant. After adding the herbs, take the pot off the heat and carefully pour the mixture into a large, heat-resistant bowl. Cover your head with a towel and lean over the bowl, with your face around 7 to 12 inches from the water's surface. (If at first the steam is too hot, you can partially uncover your head.) Breathe deeply. Continue to inhale the fragrant steam for up to ten minutes. Repeat as needed.

FOUR

Gardening

HOW TO

—

START
A VEGETABLE
GARDEN

—

"Growing your own food connects you to the soil in
a way that feeds both the body and the spirit. Every time
I plant seeds and they sprout and grow into the food
that nurtures me, I am humbled and awed by the process.
The garden offers us many lessons, among them
patience and the reminder that what fails can teach us
more than what succeeds. Just put your hands in the earth
and let the story of your garden begin."

—Lauri Kranz, Edible Gardens LA

GROWTH INVESTMENT

Setting up a little patch of soil in which your vegetables can thrive is one of the most satisfying of garden projects. Stake out your plot and start digging. Here's how.

LOCATION, LOCATION, LOCATION

The two most important things to take into consideration when starting a vegetable garden are sun and soil. Choose the area of your backyard that receives the most sun per day. With three to four hours of direct sunlight, you can successfully grow leafy greens, such as lettuce, spinach, Swiss chard, and kale, as well as a variety of herbs. In comparison, tomatoes, eggplant, corn, squash, peppers, and the like will need five or more hours of sun per day to really flourish.

GIVE YOUR PLANTS A BOOST

Once you've settled on a sunny patch, tend to the soil. Building raised beds is a great way to ensure you have healthy soil from the very beginning. They can be built on existing soil or hardscape.

On hardscape, build your beds at least 18 inches tall (approximately three wood boards), so that the roots of the plants have enough room to spread out and grow. To fill the beds, use a good organic soil and add it almost to the top. Finish with a final layer of compost to help the seeds germinate and feed the soil below when watered.

If building on existing soil, your beds can be around 12 inches high (approximately two boards), as long as you amend the soil beneath by at least 6 inches. To do this, follow the double-dig method that John Jeavons recommends in his classic book *How to Grow More Vegetables*. The basic idea behind this technique is to enrich your soil by layering rich compost and existing soil into a kind of garden lasagna. (The double-dig method is also ideal when starting your garden directly in the ground without the use of raised beds.)

A Note on Materials

Use only untreated wood—preferably cedar or redwood—since treated wood can leach chemicals into your soil and, by extension, your food.

The Ecological Art of Permaculture

A blend of the words *permanent* and *agriculture*, *permaculture* was a term born in the 1970s to describe a set of practical, integrative, holistic solutions that resemble those found in nature. In other words, working *with* the land rather than *against* it. A vegetable garden, for example, should mimic the structure of a natural forest, with a raised garden bed loosely surrounded by a careful composition of perennials, shrubs, fruit trees, and ground-hugging berry plants. Learning how to integrate the built environment with the landscape is a lesson in life as much as in gardening. Here are three tips:

- Let go
  A permaculture plot might seem an uncultivated mess compared to the well-manicured parks and lawns of urban environments. But nature has sophisticated ways of controlling insects and using sunlight. All you need to do is watch and learn.

- Think different
  Try new ways to grow. When planting seeds, make curved rows rather than straight rows, which are meant to facilitate harvesting but don't benefit the garden as a whole. Scalloped shapes naturally protect plants from wind and soil erosion, act as suntraps in clearings, and require less weeding in the unplanted areas.

- Start small
  Take one step at a time. The aim should be to reduce man power to a minimum by carefully intercropping a mix of plants, creating fertilizer rather than buying it, and storing and using minimal water for cultivation without irrigation. Nature is already perfect; you can only nuture it.

All-Natural Soil Conditioners

Animal dung has been put to use by farmers and homesteaders for centuries, providing the organic materials that build soil, thereby helping the soil hold more nutrients and water, and thus become more fertile. For those without a herd of cattle in the backyard, these all-natural soil conditioners are an ideal way to give your indoor and outdoor plants a nutritional boost without resorting to harmful chemical fertilizers. Harvested from cows and horses that graze freely, the manure is dried so that it has little to no odor and, unlike fresh manure, won't burn delicate leaves. Steep one bag (also known as "manure tea") in a five-gallon container of water for one to three days, fill up your watering can, pour over your compost, and watch your plants thrive.

GROW
A TOMATO

—

"Gardening not only brings about a sense of satisfaction,
a deep connectedness to the world, and a chance
for quiet production, it also ensures that the food you grow
has better flavor. You can truly taste the care
and wonder of the garden in every crop you yield."

—Liz Solms, Banana Tree Consulting

TOMATO, OR NOT TOMATO?

Anyone can grow a tomato plant. Hardy, versatile, and delicious, they require only a small amount of space and a whole lot of sun to thrive. It doesn't matter much whether you've got an acre of fertile land or a big pot in a sunny window.

START WITH A STARTER

We recommend kicking off your tomato garden with starter plants rather than seeds, as their hardiness allows you to transplant them more easily. When choosing a starter, which can be purchased at your local nursery, look for plants that have not yet begun to fruit or flower. The younger the seedlings, the better, as they adapt quicker after transplanting. Tomatoes come in endless variations, from sweet and tiny to big and juicy, so think about how you'd like to use your harvest. Do you want to stew them, can them, cook them, or throw them on a salad? Pick the plant that will make your culinary wishes come true.

WHO LOVES THE SUN?

Whether outdoors or indoors, make sure your tomato plants are living in a warm, bright spot that gets approximately ten hours of sunlight a day. If you don't have a sunny, south-facing window, you can use a grow light and a heating coil beneath to warm your plant from the bottom. Too little light and warmth will cause it to grow weak and pale.

GET DIGGING

Whether you're planting in a garden or a large pot, it's best to grow tomatoes in a mix of organic soil and compost. Make large holes for each starter plant, digging enough soil away to make a clear space for the root system. Cover the bottom of the hole with a scattering of compost. You can add a handful of bonemeal or a spoonful of Epsom salt, which contains the magnesium tomatoes love. Place your starter plant in the hole and fill it back in with soil until the lowest leaves are just above the soil line. Gently pat down to remove air pockets, and water deeply.

If you're planting more than one tomato plant, place the starters 2 to 4 feet apart so they have room to grow. Tomatoes grow fast and tall, and they like a little something to lean on. Now is the time to set up some sort of climbing structure. Six-foot-tall stakes work well for most tomato varieties, but a trellis is also a fine option. (Stakes can damage root systems if added later in the growing process, so set them up early.) As your plants grow, gently guide them upward by attaching the central stem to the trellis or stake with a string or garden tape.

If you're planting in a pot or raised beds, follow the same process. The larger the pot or bed, the more tomatoes you'll yield, but these hardy plants will grow even in smaller quarters. If your container is at least 1 foot deep and 1 foot wide, a tomato should be able to grow. Just make sure there are drainage holes so the water can flow through the soil and out of the container.

JUST ADD WATER

About once a week is enough watering for tomatoes—maybe a bit more if it's a particularly hot, dry summer. Water directly onto the soil, never onto the plant leaves, as that can encourage mold and disease.

SO LONG, SUCKERS

As your plant grows, don't forget to prune. Pinch off the "suckers"—the small non-fruiting branches that sprout up between the main stem and flowering branches. The fewer suckers, the more your plant can dedicate its nutrients and energy to its fruit-producing parts. As your tomatoes ripen, encourage new growth by adding an organic tomato food of your choice (available online or at most nurseries) to the soil around the bottom of the stem. Trimming upper leaves can also encourage fuller, more fruitful growth.

ENJOY THE FRUITS OF YOUR LABOR

Once your tomatoes start appearing, don't get overzealous and pick them too soon. Vine ripened is best, so wait until they are fully colored and plump to the touch before harvesting. Then, pickle, fry, dice, can, or stew them, or add a dash of salt and bite right in. Perfection.

Handmade Picking Baskets

Once your tomato plant starts to fruit, stockpile the harvest in
a handsome carrier. Made for more than a century in
New Hampshire, these utilitarian baskets are tightly woven with strong
ash and finished with suede handles. When not storing
fresh produce or grains, the containers can also be used to keep
blankets in and organize homewares.

CONTROL GARDEN PESTS NATURALLY

—

"We are all part of the web of life. It's that simple. This idea really came to the forefront for me when I started beekeeping. I saw how the pesticides we use affect not only the insects we want to eradicate but the bees, flowers, and plant life as well. We need to work in our gardens with that in mind."

—Erik Knutzen, Root Simple

BUG OFF!

Critters and crawlers can wreak havoc on a backyard garden, but there are methods to keep creatures at bay that won't harm the plants or soil. Commercial chemical pesticides can be a harsh measure, successfully killing bugs and worms but also polluting the soil and spreading disease through insect communities. Here are six tips to keeping your garden thriving without harming the environment.

SET STRONG ROOTS

When first starting your garden, make sure to use healthy, organic soil along with natural mulch and compost. Natural fertilizer and healthy dirt is the first step to growing strong plants. Also, be sure to keep your garden area clear of any weeds or yard debris, which attracts and breeds insects.

DIVIDE AND CONQUER

Carefully watch your garden as it grows, and pull out any weak plants that may be diseased or infected, removing those with dead, yellowing leaves or mold and bug infestation. Dispose of these plants in your regular trash bin, rather than back into the garden, to avoid contamination.

THE GOOD WEED

There is no better natural fertilizer than seaweed. Robust with all the goodness that makes plants strong—zinc, iron, calcium, sulfur, magnesium, and more—seaweed is a miracle worker for your backyard crops. You can use it as mulch or in liquid form to promote growth and assist plants in repelling disease and slugs. No need to be living by a coast: you can acquire a ready-made seaweed fertilizer in most gardening stores or online.

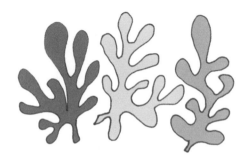

SWITCH IT UP

Rotate your crops and mix your plantings; they like variety. Pests are far less likely to infect a garden if you plant different types of veggies, flowers, and herbs, and change up where your plantings are located. Each year, rotate both what you plant and where you plant it, and avoid attracting the same old pests from seasons past in the process.

BE AN EARLY BIRD

Water your garden early in the morning, as wet leaves in high sun can cause plants to burn, and wet leaves in the evening can result in mold. Early morning waterings are best so that plants stay nourished but dry. Be sure to water the soil and not the leaves, as excess moisture attracts both insects and all sorts of unwelcome fungi. For larger gardens we highly recommend researching various methods of drip irrigation.

TIDY TOOLSHED, TIDY MIND

Clean all your gardening tools after every use to avoid spreading bugs and disease from one plant to the next. It's an easy task that will save you much trouble in the long run.

Natural fertilizer and healthy dirt is the first step to growing strong plants.

Make Your Own Natural Antipest Remedies

To combat mites, aphids, or mealybugs, try mixing 1 tablespoon of canola oil and a few drops of natural dish soap into 1 quart of water. Pour the concoction into a spray bottle, shake it up, and spritz the infected plant from top to bottom, making sure to get the undersides of the leaves, where pests like to hide. You can add baking soda, hot pepper sauce, or even cayenne to up the antipest ante.

For fungus and mildew, add 2 tablespoons of baking soda into 1 quart of water. You can also add a splash of whole milk if you're feeling especially vindictive. (The milk proteins interact with the sun to create an antiseptic effect.) Pour the mix into a spray bottle and shake, then spritz the affected areas. Repeat every few days until your plants are mildew free. (Note: Even natural pest control should stay out of reach of children and pets.)

Nature's Little Helpers

All kinds of flowers can bring bees and butterflies to a garden—both so necessary for a healthy garden and to ward off pests. Plant nasturtium flowers near cucumbers to help keep cucumber beetles away. Try oregano with squash to deter a multitude of garden pests. Plant borage flowers near your tomatoes, as they protect against hornworms and can even improve the flavor of the tomatoes. (The beautiful purple blooms of borage, an edible flower, can be tossed into a salad.) Start the flowers by seed and sow them at the same time the first vegetable seeds are planted. Make sure to water regularly, keeping in mind that both too much or too little water can kill a garden. A garden, like life, is all about balance.

SAVE
A SEED

—

"Our agrarian ancestors would be turning in their plots
if they saw us throwing away perfectly good seeds at the end
of every season, only to buy seeds of unknown origin
come spring. Become a seed saver and preserve our food
heritage while making it easy to grow better, tastier,
healthier plants at home."

—**Susan Morrell, writer and gardener**

GO BACK TO YOUR ROOTS

Saving your own seeds gives you more control over what you grow in your garden and allows you to get involved in one of nature's most essential processes. There's no need to take a chance on a new, anonymous packet from the store. Gather seeds from a delicious batch of tomatoes and enjoy them again the following year. (They get better with each season.) The same goes for peppers, morning glories, beans, or even the basil and mint in your windowsill.

Collecting seeds from heirloom or heritage plants also helps preserve biodiversity. This is because heirloom crops are open pollinated—meaning that they are pollinated naturally by insects, birds, or the wind—and therefore more genetically diverse and reliable from year to year. They've been passed down for generations, naturally adapting to the weather and pests of the surrounding region and thriving without the need for chemical fertilizers. Open-pollinated crops were the norm before mass hybridization became commonplace and commercial farmers started breeding crops to resist specific diseases and last longer on grocery shelves and in the backs of far-traveling trucks.

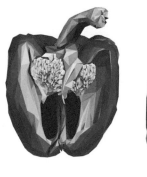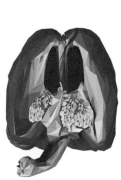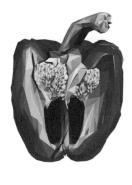

Seeds come in a variety of natural packaging: berries, nuts, pods, or the more attention-grabbing exploding seed heads. Here's how to gather yours.

GATHER AND WAIT

If left to themselves, the fleshy produce in your garden would naturally fall to the earth, where some of their seeds might sprout again when spring arrives. Saving seeds from these plants mimics this natural cycle. The key is to collect them after they've fully matured on the plant but before they've fallen off.

CHOOSE WISELY

Harvest your seeds from plants that produced well this year to provide the best genes for next year's harvest. To ensure you save seeds from the brightest, healthiest plants, tie a ribbon around the stems of your favorite blooms and most prolific veggie plants while they're still at their peak. Once they start to fade and overripen at the end of the season, you'll know where to go.

COLLECT YOUR SEED

The seeds of produce, such as peppers, tomatoes, melons, and winter squash, can be saved when the fruit or vegetable is fully ripe and ready to eat. Simply scoop out the seeds, rinse them well in a strainer, and spread them out to dry on a baking sheet or plate. (Avoid paper, as it can stick.) Keep the seeds in a cool, dry place away from direct sunlight and drafty windows. Allow a few days for them to dry completely. Tomato seeds are a special case, as the added step of fermentation is required to keep them viable. (A reliable reference can be found at howtosaveseeds.com.)

Other produce, such as eggplants, cucumbers, and summer squashes, must ripen beyond the ready-to-eat stage before their seeds mature. Wait until the produce is fleshy and soft (or in the case of eggplant, almost hard) with dull coloring. Once you've picked the produce, cut it open, scoop out the seeds, rinse them well, and dry them, following the same instructions as before.

The flavorsome green leaves of culinary herbs, such as cilantro and basil, are usually picked before any flowers sprout, but for seed-saving purposes, let a few herb plants flower and go to seed, then collect your bounty.

Instead of deadheading your flowers (the gardener's chore of popping off dead flowers to encourage continued blooms), allow a few to lose their petals, turn brown, and dry out. The flowers won't be pretty, but the seeds they leave behind for you to collect are worth their weight in gold. Simply clip the seed heads into clean, dry hands, or slip a brown paper bag over the seed head, then snip the stem and let the seedpod fall into the bag. Gently shake the seeds loose in the bag and store them in smaller packets.

KEEP THEM SAFE

Store your seeds in paper envelopes, marked with plant variety and date, inside an airtight container, such as a glass jar. Seeds may keep longer than a year, but their viability will lessen as time goes on.

For more tips on how to save seeds from a variety of flowers, fruits, and vegetables, get to know the Seed Savers Exchange (seedsavers.org).

Heirloom to the Throne

Ask anyone with a green thumb and a romantic inclination which heirloom is most important, and that person will inevitably get misty eyed over a favorite tomato. The mutations and nuances of texture and taste appear endless, and the names dreamlike: Brandywine, Cherokee purple, Zapotec pleated (a pink variety said to resemble a girl's twirling dress). The voluptuous shapes and brash colors of these fruits appear like characters from a Picasso painting, with each edible gem seemingly endowed by nature with a particular destiny: Amish paste for sauces, Chianti rose for cool weather, San Marzano for just about everything from canning to eating barefoot in the garden. That kaleidoscope of tomatoes with quaint names and unique characteristics links us back to our pioneering ancestors and preserves our agricultural heritage.

TOOL OF THE TRADE

Manila Hemp Seed Envelopes

Half the fun of seed saving is bringing out your seed envelopes when a new growing season begins, like little gifts carefully sealed and stowed away. These English Manila hemp packets with gummed seals include sections for jotting down all the essential details—date collected, variety, seed type— to pass on when sharing seeds with friends.

BUILD
A BIRDFEEDER

—

"I enjoy birding as an entertaining pastime throughout the year. Birds are creatures without boundaries. They live all over the world in every climate and environment, from the desert to the jungle. Some birds travel from one pole to the other. To be even a little bit aware of the birds around you provides insight into the flux of seasons and gives a deeper appreciation of the world around us."

—Jacob Schachter, Franklin Park Zoo

BUILD YOUR SEED CAPITAL

This simple method for building a birdfeeder—cutting a few holes in a plastic soda bottle and filling it with birdseed—isn't too far from what you might have done in elementary school art class. The vessel here, however, will last through many a season—and look good doing so, thanks to the sturdy materials with which it is made.

1 Take the smaller plank of wood and, using the Forstner bit, drill a hole in the center around 1 ½ inches in diameter. Then, to create the frame that will hold your birdfeeder, form a right angle with the two planks and use two screws to connect the pieces together. Add wood glue if you want the extra support.

→

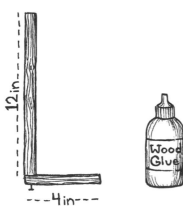

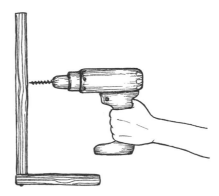

2   Hold your empty glass bottle up against the frame, with the bottle opening pointed down, about 1 ½ inches above the floor of the frame. (Keep in mind that the amount of space you leave between the floor of the feeder and the bottle opening will determine how fast the birdseed flows into the small vessel below.) Make two pencil marks on either side of the bottle where the neck starts to taper. Make two more marks a few inches below the bottom of the bottle (near the top of the frame).

3   Using those four pencil marks as guides, drill four holes just large enough to fit your wire through. Add your screw hook to the frame, on the top narrow edge of the back plank.

4   Fill your bottle with birdseed and twist on the bottle cap. Flip it upside down and position it within the frame, using your markings as a guide. Wrap the wire tightly around the bottle to hold it flush against the frame, then feed the wire through the drill holes and staple it to the back of the frame. This step is made easier with a second set of helping hands.

5   Hang your birdfeeder where you can easily see it—but away from pets and wildlife that could harass the birds. Once you've picked a spot, slip the vessel under the bottle opening and unscrew the cap (this takes a little finesse, as the vessel and the bottle are now close together), allowing the birdseed to flow out.

6   To refill, remove the vessel, unhook the feeder, and flip the frame upside down. Place a funnel in the hole of the floor and add more birdseed as needed. Then twist on the cap, rehang the feeder, and place the vessel back under the bottle before unscrewing the top and letting the bird buffet recommence!

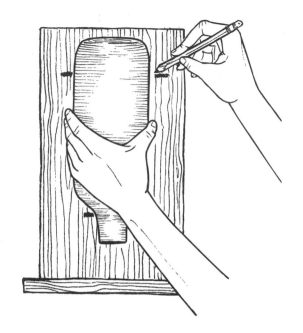

*To be even a little bit aware
of the birds around you
provides insight into the flux
of seasons and gives
a deeper appreciation of the
world around us.*

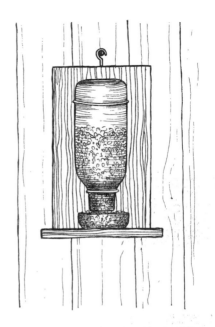

Pecking Order

The kind of seed you use will dictate what birds come calling.
Sunflower seeds are an all-around favorite with nearly every species—
just make sure to hang your feeder in a spot where you don't mind
having a pile of cracked sunflower shells. (You can solve the shell
dilemma by stockpiling the feeder with pre-hulled sunflower seeds.)
If you'd like to invite over some ravens, cranes, ducks, or jays,
use a little cracked corn. Finches and mourning doves enjoy thistle
seed, while a wide variety of birds will come to visit on the promise
of just a few scattered bits of leftover bread. Watch your feeder and
observe what your locals like—but remember to always clean up
leftovers. If bird food sits for too long, it can grow mold and bacteria
that will ultimately harm your feathered friends.

PRUNE

—

"While much of farming is hard work and somewhat monotonous, I always look forward to pruning, because it requires focus, creative thinking, and decision making. Of course, you need skill to prune, but also instinct: observe the plant and see where exactly you should make a cut. If you're in the right state of mind, pruning can be one of the most relaxing and meditative tasks."

—Vera Fabian, farm manager

MAKE A CLEAN CUT

Before performing pruning surgery on your garden patients, it's important to understand basic plant science, particularly the fact that plants do not have immune systems in the human sense of the term. When they are sick or wounded, they have a built-in capacity to "wall off," or compartmentalize the parts of themselves that are dying or ill. Always be sure to sterilize your tools after cutting or pruning, as it is possible to spread disease from one plant to another just by using a pair of dirty shears.

There are four basic pruning techniques, or cuts, each creating a different effect on plant growth and visual aesthetics.

1   Pinching is one of the simplest pruning methods and is done by pinching the terminal bud off the plant to stop the stem from growing outward and encourage new branches to grow off the stem for a more glamorous, bushier look. Pinching works best on annual and perennial flowers and veggies, and it can also help direct growth on small shrubs to maintain an even, pleasing shape.

→

2 Heading cuts are made farther back on the stem, just above a lateral bud. In most cases, the lateral bud has already grown a leaf, and you should make the cut directly above it. Handheld pruners are usually the best tool for the job, helping to stimulate buds and encourage fuller, denser growth. Heading works well on perennial flowers and small shrubbery.

3 Thinning requires handheld pruners or tools such as loppers or pruning saws to do more serious surgery in the garden. This method does exactly what its name claims: reduces the bulk of a plant by cutting away entire branches or stems. By removing lateral buds in bulk, you can keep unwanted shoots at bay and give your plants a trimmed-down look. Thinning cuts should be made right at the base of the branch to prevent it from growing back.

4 Shearing cuts are usually used to shape hedges and bushes, to give larger plants and shrubs a stylish cut, and are the method of choice for whimsical topiary projects. Shearing stimulates bud growth, so you'll find that sheared plants will grow out their haircuts faster than usual. Since this type of pruning is meant for cutting leaves as well as stems, it's best to shear small-leaf plants with handheld trimmers that allow for extra precision. Because nobody—plants included—wants a bad haircut.

Timing Is Everything

You can prune dead or diseased flowers or wood any time of the year, but try to avoid pruning in the fall, when sudden cold weather can kill a vulnerable, freshly pruned plant. In general, late winter or early spring is the perfect time to prune fruit trees, summer flowering shrubs, evergreens, and deciduous bushes and trees. Roses are usually trimmed around this turn of the season, as well as early bloomers, such as forsythia and lilacs. If your plant is a food producer, the exact timing of pruning can get tricky, so we recommend researching by region and type of plant.

TOOL OF THE TRADE

English Steel Garden Shears

Originally created for shearing sheep by hand, this version by Burgon and Ball—updated and adapted for pruning—has been produced for more than 280 years in Sheffield, England. Sharp, tempered steel and what's known as a double-bow handle make these shears ideal for the detail-oriented gardener and are perfect for a variety of uses, including heading cuts, grass clipping, foliage trimming, and topiary.

PLANT
BY SEASON

—

"Plants you've grown yourself and picked fresh from the earth have the most incredible flavor. That vibrant taste very much depends on whether your crop was planted in the right soil and at the right time. Getting the most from your garden is only possible if you pay close attention to the seasons and stay connected to the agricultural history of the land you are gardening."

—Gordon Jenkins, farmer

FIND YOUR PLACE IN THE SUN

The success or failure of your outdoor veggie and herb garden very much depends on what you plant and when you plant it. Even garden novices can get great results just by knowing how to read the simple signposts of seasons and the sun (or the phases of the moon). There are various factors to keep in mind while digging in the dirt, from the best time of year for planting to your home locale. Herewith, an overview.

1 Research your plant hardiness zone—an easy-to-understand mapping system that conveniently breaks down planting zones in different countries and regions based on average annual minimum temperatures. If you're in the United States, your zone can be found on the USDA's official Plant Hardiness Zone Map (planthardiness.ars.usda.gov).

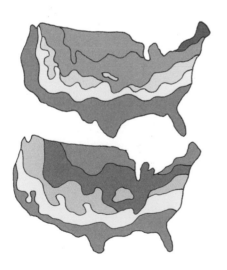

2 The general rule of (green) thumb for most planting zones is that Mother Nature will grant you a ninety-day window, give or take a few, for your garden to grow and mature. That said, think ahead and try to stay away from planting anything that might be particularly slow on the draw. If you choose a late-bloomer variety, be prepared to help it along, whether by starting your seeds indoors or by giving the plant some extra love and light in the form of a cold frame (basically a clear glass box placed over the plant, which keeps things nice and cozy). A cold frame can also extend your growing season for certain plants. If you live in a warmer climate, you can usually count on a longer growing season even without a cold frame and may be able to grow tougher plants—such as kale, carrots, hardy greens, and root vegetables—throughout the winter months.

→

3 Once you know your zone and have a general idea of what kind of plants you'd like to nurture, take a good look at your intended garden area and record how much sunlight and shade it receives each day of the growing season. You can even take a pencil and paper and map it out old school.

Here's a quick reference for planting according to the sun:

- If your garden gets full sun, meaning at least six hours of direct rays each day, read the backs of your seed packs and choose "full sun" seeds that are true sun lovers.
- If your patch only gets four or five hours of direct sun each day, grab those seeds that love "partial sun."
- Only two to four hours of sun each day? Look for the seed packs that say "partial shade."
- If you get less than an hour of sun, you need to find some goth veggie types—for example, Asian varieties such as bok choy—that prefer to hide in the shade and howl at the moon.

4 Now that you know how much sun you have, find out in which time of year in your planting zone it's best to start and how long your growing season is. Then (finally!) it's time to plant. Take a long look at your garden, map out where seed (or starter plants) should go, plant according to the directions on the seed packs, and clearly label which plants are where with seed markers. If you're in a quandary regarding the sorts of plants you'd like and where exactly you want them, here is a helpful way to remember: If you grow it for the root or fruit, you need full sun. If you grow it for the leaves, partial shade is all you need.

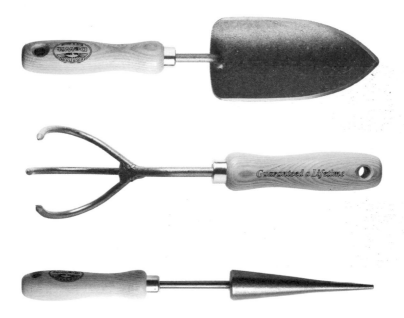

Steel-and-Ash Gardening Set

Manufactured by DeWit in the Netherlands, this trio of classic garden tools
will make any gardening job easier and add a touch of sophistication
to your kit. Plant seeds, dig holes, and claw out tenacious roots with the dibber,
trowel, and cultivator, respectively. Sturdy and sleekly designed, each
tool is made with hand-forged boron steel and ash, and handcrafted by
DeWit blacksmiths using trade secrets loyally kept since 1893.

FIVE

Grooming

HOW TO

CARE
FOR RAW
DENIM

—

"Caring for raw denim is counterintuitive: The more
you love a pair of jeans, the less you should fuss over them.
All the oils, sweat, and grime of your life will make
those jeans beautiful with age. Tracing the wrinkles in a pair
of dark indigo jeans is like discovering the story of how
each and every crease came to be. The trick is to wear your
pair as much as possible to properly break them in."

—Katrina Klein, denim designer

TWILL OF A LIFETIME

Unless you're a die-hard raw-denim fan, you'll probably choose to wash your jeans at some point. In fact, washing can better preserve the material. If your pair is blue or indigo dyed, wear them regularly for roughly six months before cleaning for the first time. Unlike black sulfur–dyed jeans, which has dye fully soaked into the fabric, indigo dye sits on top of the denim and needs time to completely absorb into the material. Wait longer than a year, however, and the crotch may rip or "blow out," meaning the grime that's collected between the denim threads can ultimately weaken the fibers.

When hand washing your raw denim, always turn your jeans inside out and lay them completely flat in the tub. While submerged in water, they form new creases more easily. (A bit of indigo dye will most likely get on your tub, but it can be washed off with a bathroom cleaner if done right away.)

1   Place your jeans flat in the bathtub and fill it with lukewarm water until the denim is fully submerged. Add in Woolite for Darks, which has special chemicals to preserve darker clothing dyes. (We're still on the lookout for an environmentally conscious alternative.) Fill the cap to the first line only; you don't need much. Swirl the water and leave your jeans submerged for about forty-five minutes, watching that they don't float to the top.

→

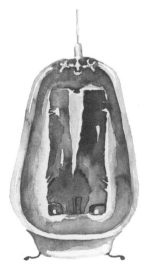

2 Drain the tub and refill again with clear water, always keeping the jeans flat on the bottom of the tub. Swish the fresh water around for a minute or so to rinse the denim. Then hang the jeans up flat and allow them to dry in the open air. This usually takes about a day. Another option during warmer months is to skip the second rinse and bring the jeans outside. Hang them up flat, hose them down, and leave them to dry outdoors, away from direct sunlight.

3 Once your raw denim has fully dried, it will feel like new again, as stiff as the first time you wore it. After a few days, it will go back to its broken-in state, but you can accelerate the process by giving your jeans a good rumble. Roll them up and throw them against your couch, wall, or floor until they break back in and become softer to the touch.

Selvedge Denim

Woven on shuttle looms with one very long, continuous cross thread moving down the length of a bolt of fabric, selvedge denim is an incredibly durable material. The production process began in the middle of the nineteenth century, when American mills used 3 yards of fabric for every pair of jeans, resulting in a denser denim. To maximize yield, the material was used right up to its "self edge" (hence the name). Red, yellow, brown, white, or green thread was stitched up the inseams, with each color representing a different weight of denim.

Deemed costly and time consuming, denim mills stopped making selvedge denim in the 1950s. Wider shuttle looms were introduced, producing a looser weave that was more prone to tearing, fraying, and fading. Even the use of indigo—the rich blue color associated with classic jeans—was replaced with a more cost-effective sulfur dye.

Sensing an opportunity, the Japanese bought many of the old machines from American mills in the 1980s. These older looms, made with cast iron and harness springs, produced bolts of selvedge with subtle imperfections and beautiful character that are impossible to mass-produce. Today, the machines create pieces for the high-end denim market and are priceless artifacts in the history of denim— not to mention the very fabric of American culture.

Denim and Canvas Waterproofing Wax

Otter Wax was invented in the home kitchen of a man who was looking for
a more sustainable, renewable way to waterproof his best clothes.
Most waterproofing substances use petroleum distillates, oil refinery by-products,
and silicone to get the job done—potentially making things oily, smelly,
and not so kind on the environment. Made from beeswax and a secret mix
of plant-based oils, this all-natural bar helps you preserve and protect
your old canvas bag, trusty denim jacket, or favorite pair of jeans the natural way.

FOLD
A POCKET
SQUARE

—

"Pocket squares have been around for generations.
What's inside that little space in your pocket can actually be
the difference between a guy wearing a nice suit and
a guy who really knows how to dress. A pocket square quiets
a loud ensemble or dresses up a drab one. Unlike the
utilitarian handkerchief, used to wipe your hands or brow
or nose, the pocket square is purely decorative. Now the
lines have blurred and each guy can have his own unique take.
That modest swatch is an avenue to express yourself."

—Jay Arem, the Knottery

KNOW HOW TO FOLD 'EM

The pocket square first made its dapper mark on the historical record in ancient Greece, when wealthy Greeks carried perfumed kerchiefs. In modern Europe, noblemen had pocket squares on hand for their delicate noses, or for a lady friend in need. Today, pocket squares deliver a stylish flourish when tucked into a suit pocket.

STYLE, SQUARED

Pocket squares are an inexpensive and easily interchangeable way to try out different styles and maybe even find a signature look. They should pick up color and texture from your tie, but they don't have to be a direct match. The coarser texture of linen pops nicely against a jacket in a smooth fabric, for example. Or, conversely, play with balance by sporting a square in lighter silk with a heavier-knit wool tie. When going for a clean, put-together look, you can't go wrong with neutral colors, such as gray, cream, or classic white. The following are three classic styles for every occasion.

POINTED FOLDS

Crisp lines are the hallmark of this group, which is best suited to cotton or linen pocket squares. Keep in mind that the more points you add, the more formal the look. One- and two-point folds look smart for business events, whereas three- and four-point folds elevate your outfit's sophistication to black-tie level.

The One-Point Fold

Fold your pocket square once horizontally and once vertically to create a smaller square, then fold that into a triangle. Fold the bottom corners into the middle to make the cloth the same width as your breast pocket, and slip inside. If done correctly, your one-point fold should look like a square house with a triangular roof.

The Two-Point Fold

Again, fold your pocket square once horizontally and once vertically to create a smaller square. Now, turn it 45 degrees to create a diamond, with the folded edge on the lower right. Bring up the bottom corner to form a triangle, with the point offset slightly to the left, about half an inch, creating a second peak. Then fold in the bottom corners until the cloth fits into your pocket.

The Three-Point Fold

Follow the steps for the two-point, but fold the bottom-left corner up toward the right, forming a third peak. Then fold the bottom-right corner in along the base. To make the four-point fold, simply bring up the bottom right as the fourth and final peak.

THE FLAT (OR STRAIGHT) FOLD

Despite its simplicity, this sharp fold has an understated sophistication. Fold your pocket square to the exact width of your breast pocket, then fold up the bottom so that when you tuck it into your pocket, just a sliver (around ½ inch) peeks out.

PUFF AND REVERSE-PUFF FOLDS

Both of these styles produce a softer, more pillowlike structure that shows off luminous printed-silk pocket squares. The puff says you're making a serious effort, but the overall effect is relaxed. To create the puff, grasp your pocket square at the middle, letting the points hang down. Pinch off about halfway down, and fold up the hanging points so that the square fits in your pocket. Adjust the puff as desired. Follow the same steps for the reverse puff, but instead of the center of the pocket square peeking out, insert it upside down, so that the hanging points peek out of your pocket like petals.

SEW A BUTTON AND MEND A HEM

—

"I started sewing because I couldn't find clothes I liked to wear or that fit properly, and I wanted to make my own. Sewing is also a meditative practice with an element of trial and error, so you have to have patience and calm. You can start with simple techniques and work your way up to making—and mending—clothing for yourself and your family."

—Kristine Karnaky, Miss KK

COMMON THREADS

A knowledge of sewing basics is always useful for administering quick wardrobe fixes, like reattaching missing buttons and mending undone hems. Inevitably, those loose ends become apparent only when you're about to wear the garment, leaving you no time for a visit to the tailor. Follow this guide, and such last-minute adjustments can be made with a steady hand and a sharp eye.

THE BUTTON

Threading a needle may seem like a simple thing, but it's a skill that takes the meditative concentration of a samurai. Cut your thread—about 2 feet in a color that matches your garment—at an angle to make it easier to slip through the needle's eye. Then pull the thread through the eye until both sides are even, and knot the ends of the thread together. Knot once more for good luck.

Find the spot where you'd like your button, and push the needle and thread all the way through from the back of the garment to the front, until the knot anchors. Slide the button down the needle and thread to meet the fabric. Once the button is exactly where you want it, push the needle down through the opposite buttonhole and up through the back of the fabric, and so on. If you have a four-hole button, look at the garment's other button thread patterns to decide whether to sew through adjacent or diagonal buttonholes. Repeat four times while leaving a small space between the garment and the button.

Once the button feels firmly attached, push the needle up through the back of the garment to the front, but not through any buttonholes. Wrap the thread tightly in the space just between button and fabric, approximately six times. Push your needle through to the back of the garment once more, then snip the thread and knot the ends together. You're officially buttoned up!

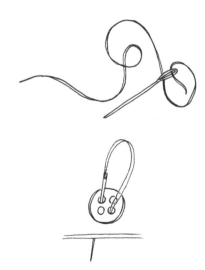

An unraveled hem can quickly be saved with your trusty needle and thread. There are several different stitches to choose from when mending a hem, but we recommend the whipstitch, which is fast and easy, creating small, nearly invisible stitches on the outside of your garment. During the entire process, keep your thread relatively loose; pulling it too tightly may pull the fabric or rip the thread. As before, it should be roughly 2 feet long and in a color that matches your garment.

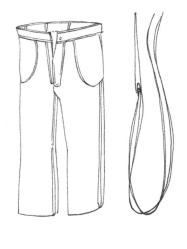

Start by turning the garment—skirt, dress, or pants—inside out, so you can work from the back of the fabric. Thread your needle as instructed before and knot the ends once. With the folded edge positioned horizontally and closer to you, place your needle about 1 inch from where the hem starts to unravel and make a small stitch to anchor the knot on the inside of the garment. Moving from right to left along the raw edge, insert the needle diagonally to the left, dipping just below the raw edge, then catch a few threads and come back up through the top of the edge. Continue in this manner, moving from right to left and keeping your stitches evenly spaced, all leaning to the right. Try to keep the movements small to create the tiniest possible stitch, so the thread will barely show on the exposed side of the fabric. When you're done, trim and knot the thread on the back of the fabric and show off your "new" threads.

Oilskin Sewing Kit

Originally referred to as a "tailor's roll" or "hussuff," this English oilskin kit was designed with the traveling tailor or seamstress in mind. Unlike clunky plastic sewing boxes, the set is easy to carry and store. It gently folds up and ties closed, and contains everything the at-home or on-the-road tailor might need: sewing needles, dressmaking pins, tape measure, and wide bow scissors.

MASTER THE AT-HOME SHAVE

—

"For me, a good shave has lots to do with process and technique. Since I run a shaving brand, my bathroom is like a shaving lab. I let the cream sit longer on my skin (around two or three minutes), and I shave with the grain everywhere. That takes a little more time and precision than some careless swipes, but it helps limit friction and, in turn, prevents irritation and razor burn— something a great barber taught me."

—Jeff Raider, Harry's

INCREASE YOUR FACE VALUE

Given that it's something a man does every morning, shaving is a simple art that should not only be carried out but also enjoyed, whether you're using a complete mug-and-brush set or keeping things straightforward with a simple razor.

SHOWER BEFORE SHAVING

Even better: shave in the shower and save that extra ten minutes for reading the paper. You'll be surprised that you don't actually need a mirror, especially if you've got a few years' experience under your belt. The shower helps open your pores and soften the hairs on your face, preventing irritation by minimizing resistance between the blade and your skin. Use your free hand to feel for any spots you might have missed. Touch up your sideburns—or, heaven forbid, your soul patch—after you dry off.

GOING WITH THE GRAIN

Everyone has a different growth pattern, and it's not necessarily the same on port versus starboard, so take some time to learn your face. The easiest way is to let your beard grow for a few days and rub your hands over your dry face. Your stubble should be pretty coarse at this point, and it will be easy to feel the path of least resistance to then follow with your razor.

OUT WITH THE OLD

As soon as your razor starts feeling dull, toss it. How do you know it's lost its edge? Check the closeness of your shave: if you see leftover hairs and your skin is irritated, your blade is dull. When in doubt, get a new one. A dull razor will do weeks' worth of damage to your face in the form of bumps that won't fade for a while. It's just not worth it.

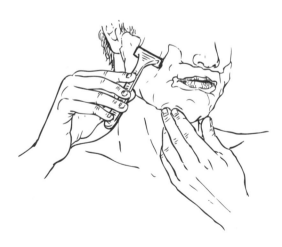

Shaving is a simple art that should not only be carried out but also enjoyed.

DON'T SKIMP

If you have the time and patience, consider a mug-and-brush kit. The brush massages your face and gets your hairs standing on end for a closer shave. When used with a quality shave soap, it's also good for creating a thick lather, which has a big impact on comfort during shaving and protecting your skin afterward. The whole process turns a daily routine into a pleasurable experience.

SLOW DOWN

Going slowly is key to avoiding nicks and razor bumps. If you're in a rush and can't shave in the shower, use warm water to rinse your razor. If you nick yourself, use a styptic pencil with some warm water to close the cut. It stings, but it works a hundred times better than that tiny, bloody piece of toilet paper still stuck to your face when you show up at work.

SPLISH SPLASH

Splash a liberal amount of warm water on your face postshave. Repeat. The warmer the water, the better to open pores and soften follicles. Follow up with a washcloth soaked in cold water to seal your pores and prevent razor burn. Dry off with a clean towel and apply your favorite aftershave—ideally something non-alcohol-based and therefore less abrasive (though a little witch hazel will work in a pinch).

TAKE A GOOD LOOK

And celebrate your well-earned handsomeness.

Close One

Want an even closer shave? See a professional. Visiting a barber for a straight-razor shave takes around forty-five minutes and is one of the most relaxing and refreshing (and affordable) grooming rituals around. These guys are trained and licensed professionals—so, gentlemen, do not try this at home. Unless, of course, you can pass the age-old test of shaving an entire balloon covered in shaving cream without popping it.

Chrome-Plated Safety Razor

You may find that this Mühle razor glides on its own heft, a feature
that sets it apart from the pop-off-cartridge and disposable-plastic models.
The closed-comb design is easier to work with than open- or slanted-
comb safety razors and far less likely to slice a vein than a straightedge.
Still, the safety razor might take some getting used to at first. Your skin
will have to adapt to the shave of the razor, and your technique
will be brought to the test—making the Mühle all the more satisfying
to master, adding a reassuring weight to your morning routine.

KNOT
AND WEAR
A TIE

—

"Every guy should learn to knot a tie, because there
is going to be a moment in his life when a tie is a must.
At that point, you are faced with the decision to
either wing it or ask for help. Don't be the guy who asks
for help—learn to tie at least one basic knot.
If you can't at all, have a cashmere V-neck on stand by."

—Katherine and Mac McMillan, Pierrepont Hicks

KNOT'S LANDING

A good tie is as well structured and timeless as the suit it complements, an accessory capable of outlasting many a seasonal trend. It serves no essential function other than decoration—and therein lies the joy. Here are two classic knots.

THE FOUR-IN-HAND

For all the ways a man can wear a necktie— and all the novelty versions he can collect for once-a-year occasions—knotting it can be summed up in three simple words: *over, under, through*. Known as the four-in-hand (so called for the drivers of four-horse carriages, who tied the reins in this same manner), this knot is the standard. For a thicker knot, upgrade to the double four-in-hand (whip it around twice).

THE WINDSOR

For a more robust knot, try the Windsor, popularized by the Duke of Windsor himself as a style that created a larger knot without the need for thicker material. But the Windsor can be taken to collar-blocking extremes; remember, bigger is not always better.

Start by holding the blade (wide end) in your left hand, hanging roughly 12 inches below the tail (narrow end), which is in your right hand. Cross the blade over the tail, then bring it up through the loop between your collar and the tie, and back down and over. Pull the blade under the tie and to your left, so that it's inside out if you're facing the mirror, then bring it across the front from your left to right. Pull the blade up through the loop again and down through the knot once more. Tighten the knot up to your collar and admire your handiwork.

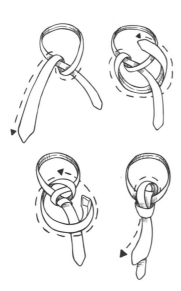

If wearing a traditional tie has lost its appeal, here are a few ways to usurp the norm:

1 Allow the tail (the thin bit of the tie that is normally tied up shorter than the front) to hang lower than the blade, once tied. Some buck convention intentionally, leaving the tail trailing rakishly in a dare-you-to-mention-it move.

2 Though stereotypically used as sartorial shorthand for geek or big-night dressing, bow ties have a practical function. The neckwear of choice for doctors and old-timey gas station attendants, a bow tie stays in place when the wearer leans over, rather than dipping into open bodies or moving gears. It makes an unexpected choice for everyday wear.

3 When you need to get down to work, be it stacking wood or simply marking up a document at the office, keep your tie out of the way by clubbing it (that is, neatly tucking it into your shirt between the first and second visible buttons). For extra panache, arch your tie by puffing it out from your shirt, sweater, or waistcoat, and pulling up the material under the knot to project like a pelican's neck. A flat-lying "noose" is all of a sudden boring in comparison.

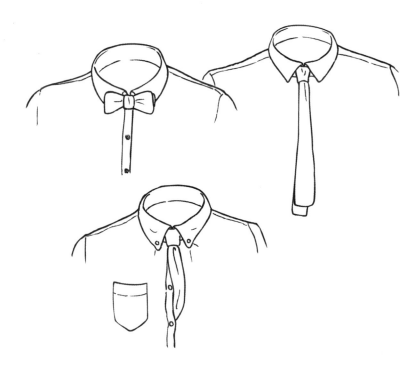

Earn Your Stripes

Regimental- or club-striped silk ties feature color schemes from the uniforms of England's traditionally all-male boarding-school system. As alumni, "old boys" would wear their school ties as a calling card. In a tight situation (say, in need of a drink but having forgotten a wallet), they might scan the room for a familiar striped tie. Regimental ties always have the stripe running from left to right, from heart to sword. Generic striped ties (often referred to as "repp" ties for their tight weave) should be striped from right to left to avoid any unintentional affiliation. To confuse matters further, American institutions usually also stripe their ties from right to left, though Anglophile Ivy League schools follow the British custom.

A good tie is as well structured and timeless as the suit it complements.

ORGANIZE
A CLOSET

—

"The key to storing and organizing both new and
vintage garments can be summed up in three simple Cs:
clean, cotton, and concede. Make sure your clothing
is clean before you put it away. Use a cotton garment bag,
or another breathable material, to store it in. And
concede that your clothing may fade a little, something may
need to be stitched or repaired, and a moth hole
may appear. But ultimately, these small imperfections
add character to your wardrobe."

—Hillary Justin, Bliss and Mischief

TAME AN UNRULY CLOSET

Closets come in all sizes and degrees of disarray, but following these simple pointers will help you tackle any organizing job.

TAKE STOCK

Open your closet and make an honest assessment: Do you really need those jeans that haven't fit since 2002? Is that Christmas sweater only there for nostalgia's sake? Clear out the sartorial cobwebs (or actual ones, if it's been a while since you've stuck your head in there). Try pairing pieces to create a few easy outfits, and donate or toss accordingly.

HANG IN THERE

Start your overhaul with proper hangers—lots of them, in uniform shape, size, and material. Wooden hangers tend to be the sturdiest, and hangers with additional clips are kindest to pants and skirts. In general, hang and group clothing by style or color. This method is not only easy on the eyes, it will also help speed up your selection process on groggy workweek mornings.

EVERYTHING IN ITS PLACE

Before you start enjoying your newly pared-down closet, take a good look at it while it's still empty. How can you best utilize the space? Do you need shelving, stacked cubicles, shoe racks? Make sure you store clothes, accessories, and shoes where you can see them. You're guaranteed to forget about anything hidden away in a corner. If you don't use it, let it go!

STORE YOUR CLOTHES THE RIGHT WAY

An empty closet and plan of attack are nothing without proper execution. Before you fill your closet back up, follow these tips for getting your things where and how they should be.

SHOES

Store shoes with the right toe and left heel out, so you'll have a clear idea of whether the sole and toe shape will look good with a certain cut of pant or length of hem. You can organize shoes like clothing, by color or style (sneakers, galoshes, boots, etc.).

SWEATERS

Cedar naturally keeps moths and other pests away—and smells much more pleasant than mothballs. Choose cedar hangers or cedar chips to store your sweaters and other cashmere and wool items. Be sure to fold your sweaters—never hang them, as this causes them to lose their shape.

PANTS AND SKIRTS

Hang pants and skirts with clip hangers to keep them neat and uniform. Skirts can be hung from the waistband. Fold pants lengthwise and hang them from the bottom cuffs to avoid marking the fabric or creating a permanent crease across the pant legs.

DITCH THE PLASTIC

Cotton and other breathable garment bags are best for storing special items, as plastic may encourage mold or moths. If you dry clean your clothes, remove the plastic bags as soon as you return from the cleaner; the chemicals from the dry cleaning process can destroy delicate fibers.

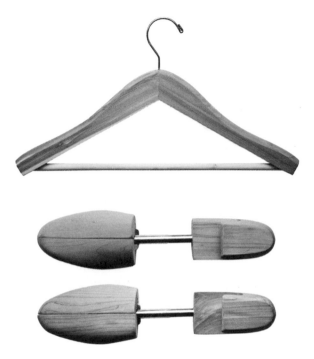

Cedar-Wood Garment Hangers and Shoe Trees

The aroma of cedar naturally repels moths and insects, and also deodorizes. The unvarnished material absorbs sweat and moisture from just-worn shoes and outerwear, helping to preserve them through the seasons. The hangers are durable enough to hold heavier clothing and are an inexpensive alternative to building an entire closet out of cedar. Carefully shaped at the toes and heels, the shoe trees maintain the original form of your footwear. Both products are turned from the scrap wood of eastern aromatic red cedar, a tree indigenous to the Northeast, by a small New Hampshire manufacturer.

PACK SMART FOR A TRIP

—

"My strategy for any long-haul trip: be prepared. The more time you spend packing and organizing at the beginning of your journey, the less time you'll spend fretting upon arrival. Ultimately, maximum preparation means maximum relaxation."

—Lizzie Garrett Mettler, *Tomboy Style*

THE CARRY-ON

When you have mere inches of personal space, compartmentalizing is your best friend. Packing compartments—structured, rectangular kit bags with zippers along three sides—are trusty travel companions that help you avoid rifling through everything once you're seated. Bring a few in your carry-on to separate toiletries and clothing. A few essentials you should keep on hand are lavender essential oil to dab on temples and behind your ears and neck, a toothbrush and travel-size toothpaste, a change of underwear and extra T-shirt (in case—gulp—your luggage goes missing), loose-fitting socks, and a thin but warm sweater in wool or cashmere.

Ideally your carry-on has a zippered top to prevent things from spilling out if the bag needs to be set on its side for storage. An extra-sturdy bottom that's shaped to sit upright and lined with a durable material, such as waxed canvas or leather, also makes travel life easier.

LEADERS OF THE PACK

The following are five effortlessly stylish staples for men and women.

THE CHELSEA BOOT

The Chelsea boot is a classic all-season shoe that can be dressed up or down in black or dark brown leather (or in neutral leopard print, for the more sartorially adventurous). The elastic ankle makes for easy removal, allowing you to slip the boots on and off at airport security and during longer flights, train rides, and car trips.

THE WHITE AND/OR BLACK JEANS

Both all-black or all-white jeans pair well with pretty much everything, from a soft cotton T-shirt to a crisp dress shirt. Unlike your regular blue jeans, they can also pass for dressier attire when worn with a simple belt, nice shoes, and a spiffed-up jacket.

THE STRIPED SHIRT

The French-style cotton sailor's shirt in white and navy stripes is remarkably versatile. Sport it at the beach with shorts, to a work function under a blazer, or in the evening with simple jewelry. The nautical stripes complement subtle patterns, so you can layer on a few colorful accessories.

THE FIELD COAT

The basic design of this coat seems made for travel: multiple pockets on the outside hold and organize your everyday items, such as a phone and keys, and hide the more touristy items, such as maps and cameras. (Carry your wallet, passport, and important documents in the breast pocket for safekeeping.) Traditionally cut from a flexible yet sturdy canvas, the field coat maintains its structure while being soft enough to roll up as a makeshift pillow.

THE SCARF

A scarf finishes off any outfit, whether in lightweight cashmere or simple cotton, depending on the season. Try a longer style that can be wrapped and knotted around your neck for extra warmth on chilly nights or worn loose during the day for a more relaxed look.

Canvas-and-Leather Weekend Bag

The two-night getaway takes much of the guesswork out of packing.
Only so many weather patterns can roll in, and only so many different events
can be had that require a whole new set of clothes. The weekend bag,
then, is meant to hold just the essentials. It should fit in an overhead compartment
or the trunk of a small car. This canvas weekender with home run leather
trim is loosely modeled after a doctor's bag (who else is as ready to pick up and
go at a moment's notice?), featuring a structured opening so you can
easily find your book or extra sweater.

CARE
FOR DELICATE
FABRICS

—

"A friend gave me a beautiful cashmere blanket as a present,
and that's how I started my collection. I was always
inherently drawn to cashmere. It's versatile and functional.
The texture of the fabric is incredibly tactile, and
you can really control the thickness with hand-spun yarn.
The end result is something that is both utilitarian
and the ultimate luxury."

—Greg Chait, the Elder Statesman

HANDLE WITH CARE

Fine fabrics require a special touch and should always be washed by hand in a clean sink. Here's how to care for silk, wool, cashmere, and leather.

SILK

Soft and smooth to the touch, silk is also one of the most enduring natural materials out there. It's stronger than steel and more flexible than nylon. Silk is sensitive to anything alkaline, meaning, you need to keep your silks away from borax, washing soda or baking soda, and all lye-based soaps.

Wet Wash for Silk

1 Fill the sink with cool, fresh water.
2 Add a capful of a mild, castile-based soap that won't strip the natural oils in silk. High-quality hair shampoo can also work. Splash the water so it foams a bit.
3 Gently hand swirl your garment in the soapy water, being careful not to wring or twist the fabric. Silk responds best to a loving touch. Wash in this manner for three to five minutes, then rinse with cool water.
4 If your silks have a particularly stubborn stain, a splash of white vinegar or lemon juice can help. Mix a tablespoon of the lemon juice or vinegar with a tablespoon of cool water. Pour the mixture directly on the stain and rub gently. Test for colorfastness on a hidden hem before trying this method on an exposed part of the silk garment.
5 With the lightest of hands, press water out of the fabric (again, no twisting or wringing) and hang the silk on a padded hanger or lay it flat to dry.

WOOL

Unlike fur or hair, wool fibers have a microscopic outer layer that prevents water from penetrating. At the same time, the fiber has the capacity to wick away sweat from the body, keeping the wearer warm and dry. Like silk, wool can be ruined by baking sodas or harsh, lye-based soaps.

Wet Wash For Wool

1 Fill the sink with lukewarm water, around room temperature, so as not to shrink the fabric.
2 Add a capful of a mild detergent with a pH below 7. Choose natural detergents especially made for wool or a mild natural baby shampoo.
3 As with silk, gently swirl the wool through the foaming water, being careful not to wring or twist the fabric. Wash in this way for three to five minutes and rinse with cool water.
4 To spot-clean stains, mix a tablespoon of lemon juice or white vinegar with a tablespoon of cool water and apply directly to the stain. Rub gently. As always, test for colorfastness on a hidden hem beforehand.
5 Gently press water out of the fabric. You can shape the wool before drying by laying the garment out flat on a towel and carefully stretching it to the desired shape and size.
6 Air-dry your wool by laying the fabric flat (hanging will stretch most wool garments) and allow it to dry—in sunlight, if possible. The sun's rays help to keep wool fluffy and fresh, repelling moths and deodorizing with its ultraviolet rays. But be aware that too much sun can fade colors.

CASHMERE

Cashmere is woven of the softest goat's-hair yarn, the ultimate luxury fabric. If your cashmere has begun to pill, don't fret. Prior to washing, you can use a pumice sweater stone to remove the pills. Another method is to simply comb the fabric gently with a clean boar-bristle brush.

Wet Wash For Cashmere

1 Fill the sink with lukewarm water, at around room temperature.
2 Add a capful of an all-natural washing detergent specifically made for cashmere, or a mild natural baby shampoo.
3 Put your clothing in the sink and, with your hands, gently press soapy water through the cashmere, being careful not to wring or twist the fabric. Wash in this manner for three to five minutes. When done, rinse with clear, cool water.
4 Gently press water out of the fabric.
5 Air-dry your cashmere by laying it on a flat surface, far away from heat sources or sunlight, which can fade the color in delicate cashmere yarn.

LEATHER

Leather is resilient and durable, yet supple. The material is relatively low maintenance. A lint-free cloth, some warm water, and a splash of mild natural detergent is all you need to remove most stains. Just work your cloth in small circles over the leather and lay it out to dry.

Every six months or so, your leather goods need an intense oil treatment to keep the material from cracking and protect it from water and weather. For best results, be sure that any treatments you use are natural.

Neatsfoot Oil

Produced from cattle hooves, this dense, moisturizing oil is used most often on baseball gloves and saddles. The oil gives leather a silky feel and the soft yellow hue darkens over time.

Mink Oil

In cream or liquid, this is the most commonly used leather oil. Moisturizing and protective, mink oil adds a reddish coloring to leather and can be mixed with waxes for additional water-proofing.

Leather Dressings

Usually used after oiling, dressings help keep dirt out while sealing moisture in.

SUEDE

Originally used for women's gloves, suede is extra soft and supple. It needs more care than regular, full-grain leather because its delicate texture and open pores are more susceptible to absorbing liquids and dirt. A few simple methods will help to keep your suede looking near new:

Waterproof

To waterproof, use a natural spray made specifically for suede. If your jacket, hat, or shoes do get wet, avoid the temptation to use heat—

blow-drying or setting your boots by the fire will only further damage the material due to drying and cracking. Instead, lay your garments out to dry away from heat or sunlight.

Brush

If your suede is dirty or matted, try a soft-bristle brush (an old toothbrush works just fine) to brush out the dirt and oils and keep it lush. For stains, try a "suede eraser" (available online and at most cobblers) to rub pesky spots away. Regular pink school erasers have a similar effect and also work well.

Steam

To restore older suede's luxurious nap and texture, steam it clean. Hold the piece a foot or more over a pot of boiling water for just a few seconds, then brush the suede thoroughly.

TOOL OF THE TRADE

Pine-and-Cast-Iron Pulley Airer

Hanging clothes to dry is not only ecologically and fiscally wise (save the environment *and* money on gas and electric bills) but also the best way to dry delicate fabrics. Inspired by a design developed during the Victorian era, this traditional ceiling-mounted laundry rack is manufactured in England using kiln-dried Scandinavian pine and cast iron. Its unique rope and double-pulley system allows you to easily raise and lower your laundry—up to 17 pounds—and is the perfect solution for indoor clothes drying in smaller spaces.

MAKE SOAP

—

"I find it very therapeutic to make soap. It's definitely
a process, consisting of a little bit of math, a little bit of science,
and a whole lot of creativity. Every time I make a batch,
I'm really kept in the moment. I think that's why I decided to
make soap for a living. I want to create things that
make a person feel good—physically, mentally, and spiritually.

—Jennifer Alden, Naked Eye Beauty

THE TRUTH ABOUT LYE

Almost all soap is made with potassium hydroxide, better known as lye. Lye reacts with fats and oils, creating a chemical combination that transmutes the ingredients into soap. Lye can be caustic and harmful if handled incorrectly. The soap-making process here starts with a safe, lye-free, premade glycerin base, which you can purchase at most craft and natural-food stores.

GET INTO THE MIX

The recipe below is among the simplest of methods for making soap and allows you to play around with color and scent. When choosing your essential oils, try a variety of combinations. Rose and lilac are soothing and fragrant. Lavender, chamomile, and tea-tree oils are healing and antibacterial. Peppermint, rosemary, and eucalyptus all serve as pick-me-ups on gray days.

- 1 pound block of natural glycerin
- Essential oils (the more you add, the stronger the scent)
- Herbs of your choice
- Stir spoon (stainless steel is best)
- Sharp carving knife or cleaver
- Double boiler
- Molds of your choice (you can use traditional soap molds or cupcake and muffin tins)

1   Cut the glycerin into 1-inch pieces and place these in the top half of the double boiler.

2   Melt the glycerin on low heat, stirring gently. Keep stirring throughout the following steps, but always with a steady hand. You don't want to create air bubbles in the soap, which will cause the mixture to foam.

3   Add the essential oils of your choice a drop at a time, until you've created your desired scent. You can also mix in fresh or dried herbs for added scent and visual punch, or natural exfoliating agents, such as soothing oatmeal and invigorating coffee grinds.

4   Carefully pour your melted mixture into your mold or tin and allow it to cool for about two hours.

5   Remove the soap from the molds. You can wrap it in tissue paper and store in a dark, dry place for later use or as a thoughtful handmade gift.

In a Lather

Historians believe the word *soap* derives from the ancient Roman temple at Mount Sapo, where animals were regularly sacrificed. Animal fat would run down the mountain into the nearby Tiber River and combine with fire ash to form a substance that women, innocently washing their clothes on the river's banks, found particularly handy for cleaning. There are even earlier appearances of soaplike substances. Babylonians boiled fats and acids for primitive hair gels, and the ancient Gauls concocted a similar mixture to use as a hair dye. In fact, most early soaps were used as pomades and styling products. The Dark Ages put a stop to all the primping and preening, and it wasn't until much later that soaps began to appear again in a variety of forms—most combined animal or vegetable fats with ash or sodium.

Contributors

EXPERTS

MICHAEL RUHLMAN is the author of more than twenty books, including *Ruhlman's Twenty: 20 Techniques, 100 Recipes, a Chef's Manifesto*, which won a 2012 James Beard Foundation Award.

CHRIS SHERMAN runs Island Creek Oysters, an oyster farm and wholesale and distribution company based in Duxbury, Massachusetts. Their oysters enjoy love affairs with many of the world's best chefs, including a long-standing residency at Thomas Keller's restaurants the French Laundry and Per Se.

BECKY SUE EPSTEIN is an award-winning author, journalist, and consultant in the fields of wine, spirits, food, and travel. She is also the author of five books, including *Champagne: A Global History* and *Brandy: A Global History*.

SOPHIA ROSE is a folk healer, herbalist, and founder of La Abeja Herbs. She conducts classes on plant medicine and traditional foods, handcrafts a line of herbal apothecary goods, and offers plant-medicine ceremonies and consultations.

TAYLOR MARDIS KATZ is a poet and farmer living in central Vermont. With her partner she runs Free Verse Farm, a small farm specializing in culinary herbs, tisanes, and herbal remedies. You can find her online at panacheperhaps.com.

TOM MYLAN is the author of *The Meat Hook Meat Book* and the founder of the Meat Hook, a butcher shop in Brooklyn. His current obsessions include mycology and clean country living.

DERRICK SCHNEIDER is a freelance writer and computer programmer living in Berkeley, California, the home of California cuisine. He writes about food and wine (and computers!) for a variety of publications.

LANCE SCHNORENBERG has worked in coffee for the last ten years as a barista, roaster, and consultant. He started Lofted Coffee Roasters in January 2014. When he's not roasting, Lance can be found building ukuleles and guitars.

BRANDON DAVEY is a bar owner and artist living and working in Brooklyn. He moved to New York for his master's degree in sculpture and developed a passion for hospitality. In 2015 Brandon opened the Topaz, a bar focused on imaginative cocktails and small-plate pairings.

JODY WILLIAMS is a New York–based chef and the founder of Buvette Gastrothèque, located in New York and Paris. She also cofounded the West Village restaurant Via Carota. Her cookbook, *Buvette: The Pleasure of Good Food*, was published in 2014.

KELLY GEARY is the author of *Tart and Sweet: 101 Canning and Pickling Recipes for the Modern Kitchen* and founder of Sweet Deliverance, a CSA-based meal-delivery service and preserves company in Brooklyn. In her spare time, she makes cooking zines, carves wooden spoons, goes to rock shows, and dreams of a house in the country.

CASS DAUBENSPECK lives in Brooklyn, where she drinks Lillet and eats cheese as often as possible.

KEITH HOBBS serves as the operations division administrator for the Idaho Department of Parks and Recreation. He began his career providing campfire programs to park visitors and has now spent twenty-four years encouraging people to enjoy the outdoors in a state park.

DAYYAN ARMSTRONG is a captain and founder of Sailing Collective, a New York–based travel company organizing adventure sailing vacations on premier charter boats in more than twenty locations worldwide. Find out more at sailingcollective.com.

THOMAS CALLAHAN is the founder of Horse Cycles. Headquartered in Williamsburg, Brooklyn, his custom bike shop makes each trusty steed by hand, from track bikes to city cruisers—a process overseen by full-time shop cat, Charles.

TRISTAN GOOLEY is a writer and navigator. He founded his natural navigation school in 2008 and is the author of two of the world's only books covering natural navigation. Find him at naturalnavigator.com

AMANDA WEBER has been the office manager for Iverson Snowshoes for four years and an avid snowshoer for more than twenty. When she's not keeping Iverson's offices in check, she enjoys spending time with her son, Dominick.

ROB GORSKI, MD, is a board-certified emergency physician actively practicing in New York. He is also a cofounder of Rabbit Island, a remote artist residency on a 91-acre island on Lake Superior.

HANK SHAW runs the site honest-food.net, nominated for the Individual Food Blog award by the James Beard Foundation. He is the author of *Hunt, Gather, Cook: Finding the Forgotten Feast* and *Duck, Duck, Goose: The Ultimate Guide to Cooking Waterfowl, Both Wild and Domesticated.*

CHRIS BURKARD is a self-taught photographer and artist whose work is layered by surf, outdoor, lifestyle, and travel subjects. He resides in central California with his wife and two sons. See more of his work at chrisburkard.com

MICKEY MELCHIONDO is better known by his stage name, Dean Ween. A fisherman, guitarist, and formerly one-half of the alternative rock group Ween, he now runs a fishing-guide service, Mickey's Guide Service, and plays in numerous bands. Find him at mickeysfishing.com

JED MAHEU is a musician, actor, and chef. He plays in the rock band Zig Zags, cooks at some of Los Angeles' best restaurants, and spends his spare time mastering the art of smoking meat.

MAC KOHLER is a New Yorker who cooks at the home end of his bike route and runs Brooklyn Copper Cookware at the business end. When not thinking about dinner, he produces his wife's music and supports subversive art.

CERISE MAYO is the founder of Nutshell Projects, a small-farm and food consultancy based in New York. Find out more at nutshellprojects.com

EXPERTS

LINDSAY COULTER joined the David Suzuki Foundation almost a decade ago, with a degree in zoology and a passion for nature. As David's Queen of Green, she leads change at the family and community level by inspiring others to live lighter and choose greener.

STEPHANIE BARTRON, APLD, is a Los Angeles–based landscape designer and has been the principal of SB Garden Design since 2000. She specializes in designing sustainable, contemporary residential gardens that are beautiful and bountiful while restoring ecosystem functionality to urban landscapes. In 2012 she coauthored Los Angeles County's *The Drought Tolerant Garden*.

SHAUN WALLACE is a woodworker and builder. He founded Gopherwood Design/Build to focus on his work as an artisan after several years in visual merchandising for a number of national retailers. Find out more at gopherwooddesignbuild.com

LISA PRZYSTUP is a florist and writer living in Brooklyn. She's an avid composer of lists of all kinds and a professional flower schlepper. You can find her work at jamessdaughterflowers.com.

AMY JO DIAZ is an artist, illustrator, and production designer. Her work can be found at iloveamyjo.com.

WENDY POLISH has a decade of experience designing in a variety of mediums. After years of experimentation with an underwater wax process invented by her father in the 1960s, Wendy cofounded the boutique candle company le Feu de l'Eau in 2011.

CASEY DZIERLENGA is a lady woodworker who has been creating sparse, whimsical designs for the past five years. See more at dzierlenga.com

MELINDA JOY MILLER is an author, gardener, medicine woman, feng shui master, and the founder of the Shambhalla Institute, which can be found at shambhallainstitute.com.

LAURI KRANZ builds, plants, and sustains organic vegetable gardens for families, chefs, schools, museums, and anyone with an interest in growing their own food through her Los Angeles–based company, Edible Gardens LA. Her work can be found at ediblegardensla.com.

LIZ SOLMS leads Banana Tree Consulting, a company based in Jamaica, with a mission to assist hotels, small farms, and private villas in establishing organic gardens and connecting to the local agricultural system. Find out more about her work at bananatreeconsulting.com.

ERIK KNUTZEN runs the site rootsimple.com and is the coauthor of *The Urban Homestead: Your Guide to Self-Sufficient Living in the Heart of the City* and *Making It: Radical Home Ec for a Post-Consumer World*. He is a cofounder, with Mark Stambler and Teresa Sitz, of the Los Angeles Bread Bakers.

SUSAN MORRELL is an American journalist living in the shadow of the Guinness brewery in Dublin, Ireland. When she's not saving seeds, she writes about travel, food, and sustainable living.

JACOB SCHACHTER is a zookeeper at the Franklin Park Zoo in Boston. He loves animals of all kinds but is particularly honored to work with birds.

VERA FABIAN is the assistant farm manager at Transplanting Traditions Community Farm in Chapel Hill, North Carolina.

GORDON JENKINS is a farm hand at Maple Spring Gardens in Cedar Grove, North Carolina.

KATRINA KLEIN lives in Brooklyn and has been designing denim for premium brands ever since she got her start with J Brand more than ten years ago.

JAY AREM is a menswear designer living in Brooklyn. When he's not looking for parking, he's running his accessories company, the Knottery. Find out more at knottery.com.

KRISTINE KARNAKY, or MissKK as she is better known, is a clothing designer, costumer, and seamstress living in Los Angeles. She can be found at misskk.com.

JEFF RAIDER is a cofounder and co-CEO of Harry's, a line of high-quality, reasonably priced men's grooming products. He is committed to creating products and brands that improve people's daily lives and building companies that positively impact the broader community.

KATHERINE AND MAC MCMILLAN are based in Brooklyn, where they run the neckwear purveyor Pierrepont Hicks as well as the American-made market Northern Grade.

HILLARY JUSTIN worked as a commercial fashion designer for nearly a decade before cofounding her successful vintage clothing business, Just Say Native. In 2014 she launched her own line, Bliss and Mischief. See more at blissandmischief.com.

LIZZIE GARRETT METTLER is a freelancer writer based in Los Angeles. She is also the founder of the blog *Tomboy Style*, which she continues to write regularly, and the author of the book of the same name. When she's not writing or blogging, she loves to hike the trails of Griffith Park.

GREG CHAIT is the founder of the Elder Statesman, a Los Angeles–based luxury lifestyle label established in 2007. Initially launched with a series of custom blankets, the brand has expanded its offering to a wide range of products. See more at elder-statesman.com.

JENNIFER ALDEN, founder of Naked Eye Beauty, is a longtime makeup artist and hair stylist. Her line uses only ingredients sourced from fair-trade-certified and organic American wholesalers, as well as her own personal organic herb and flower garden. Find out more at nakedeyebeauty.com

CONTRIBUTING WRITERS

JESSIE KWAK is a freelance writer living in Portland, Oregon, who likes to write about the good life: travel, outdoor adventures, food and beverage, and, of course, cycling. Her work can be found at jessiekwak.com.

JOHN PEABODY is a writer, photographer, and blogger at *The Hand & Eye*. When he's not working, he's usually looking for waves somewhere in the Northeast.

JAMES FOX has spent his life shuttling between southern Vermont and the Scottish Borders. From that upbringing came an equal appreciation for tweed as well as Americana. He now works with the digital libraries of some of your favorite artists and brands.

JENNIFER S. LI is a Los Angeles–based art writer and curator. When not in a museum or gallery, she is at home tending to her compost pile or camping in the wilds of California. Find out more at jenli.me.

THOMAS FRICILONE is a writer living in Brooklyn. A self-proclaimed trendsetter who often wears hats, he enjoys coffee, American literature, and general vagabonding.

EMMA SEGAL is a multitasking designer, illustrator, production consultant, well-being advocate, writer, and pilates and yoga instructor. She holistically binds these disciplines together with a passion for sustainability and health, which informs all aspects of her life and her work with clients. Find out more at emmapatricia.com.

JERID GOODING is the business partner and manager of legendary New York artist Ron Gorchov. When not coordinating international exhibitions, Jerid can be found riding around his Brooklyn neighborhood on a Pashley Guv'nor. An avid cyclist, he has raced road, cyclo-cross, and mountain bikes at a national level and worked as a shop mechanic for many years. Find him at jeridgooding.com.

DREW HUFFINE is a winemaker and writer living in Oakland, California. He and his wife make and sell small lots of handcrafted wines under their label, Trail Marker Wines. Before becoming a winemaker, Drew was an English professor in Los Angeles.

GIOVANNA MASELLI is a creative writer living in New York. She is the cofounder of *Rockaway Summer*, a local publication in the Rockaway peninsula, and a regular contributor to *Vogue Italia*. Her work has also appeared in *Elle* and the *Guardian*, among many others.

SOPHIE WISE is a fashion writer and stylist who grew up in New York and thinks the best vintage denim comes from Brooklyn vintage shops Worship, Fox and Fawn, and Grand Street Bakery. She loves cooking and Rockaway Beach.

ILLUSTRATORS

CHRISTINE MITCHELL ADAMS is an illustrator living in Burlington, Vermont. She likes to illustrate scenes and characters inspired by the culture and lifestyle of New England. Her work can be found at christinemitchelladams.com.

TY WILLIAMS is a mixed-media artist who has spent the better half of his life living out of suitcases in search of the perfect summer. When he is not surfing, he can be found indulging in exotic indigenous foods and building his world-music catalog.

HALLEY ROBERTS is an art director, photographer, and maker of breakfasts living in San Francisco. When she is not hunting for mushrooms across the West Coast, Halley can be found crawling on dirt in her garden, concocting new home remedies, and taking deep breaths. Look for her work at halleyroberts.com.

LUCY ENGELMAN is an illustrator in the most traditional sense of the word. She has had the opportunity to work with a great selection of clients, including *Bon Appetit* and *Lucky Peach*, as well as being the illustrator on staff for *Collective Quarterly* magazine. Originally calling Chicago home, Lucy spends her days exploring the duneland shores and woods of Michigan. She is easily tempted by the world outside her studio window and often prefers working among the trees.

STEFAN KNECHT is a Brooklyn-based graphic designer, illustrator, and woodworking enthusiast. He enjoys skateboarding and sketching out new tattoos. His work can be found at stefanknecht.com.

EDITORS

ALEXANDRA REDGRAVE is a writer and editor hailing from Nova Scotia, Canada. Before joining Kaufmann Mercantile as editorial director, she was the associate editor at the award-winning travel magazine *enRoute* and, later, a fellow at the Writers' Institute in New York, working with esteemed editors from *Harper's*, the *New Yorker*, and more. When not at her desk, Alex is happiest exploring— whether backpacking around Southeast Asia, driving a 37-foot lime-green RV across the United States, or shuttling across seven time zones on the Trans-Siberian Railway.

JESSICA HUNDLEY is an LA-based journalist, author, and filmmaker. She writes for publications such as *GQ*, *L'Uomo Vogue*, the *New York Times*, *Salon.com*, the *Guardian*, and many more. She directs documentaries, music videos, and commercials, and has written and edited several books, including *Dennis Hopper: Photographs 1961-1967* and *Grievous Angel: An Intimate Biography of Gram Parsons*. She is currently developing the latter into a feature-length biopic and is also in production on a feature-length animated movie, which she cowrote. Find out more at jessicahundley.com.

PUBLISHED BY
Princeton Architectural Press
202 Warren Street
Hudson, New York 12534

Visit our website at www.papress.com

ISBN: 978-1-61689-399-6

EDITOR: Tom Cho
DESIGN: Paul Wagner, Dominick Volini for Kaufmann Mercantile
DESIGN ASSISTANCE: Mia Johnson, MaryAnn George

SPECIAL THANKS TO: Nicola Brower, Janet Behning,
Erin Cain, Megan Carey, Carina Cha, Barbara Darko,
Benjamin English, Jan Cigliano Hartman, Jan Haux,
Lia Hunt, Stephanie Leke, Diane Levinson, Jennifer Lippert,
Jaime Nelson, Rob Shaeffer, Sara Stemen, Marielle Suba,
Kaymar Thomas, Joseph Weston, and Janet Wong of
Princeton Architectural Press —Kevin C. Lippert, publisher

Library of Congress Cataloging-in-Publication Data
available upon request